THE TEA
ENTHUSIAST'S
HANDBOOK

THE TEA ENTHUSIAST'S HANDBOOK

A Guide to Enjoying the World's Best Teas

Mary Lou Heiss and Robert J. Heiss

TEN SPEED PRESS
Berkeley

Copyright © 2010 by Mary Lou Heiss and
    Robert J. Heiss
Studio photographs copyright © 2007, 2010
    by Angie Cao
Location photographs copyright © 2010 by
    Mary Lou Heiss and Robert J. Heiss

Published in the United States by Ten Speed
Press, an imprint of the Crown Publishing
Group, a division of Random House, Inc.,
New York.
www.crownpublishing.com
www.tenspeed.com

Ten Speed Press and the Ten Speed Press
colophon are registered
trademarks of Random House, Inc.

Library of Congress Cataloging-
in-Publication Data
Heiss, Mary Lou.
A guide to enjoying the world's best teas /
Mary Lou Heiss and Robert J. Heiss. — 1st ed.
    p. cm.
Includes index.
Summary: "A guide offering concise,
authoritative advice on understanding, buy-
ing, and enjoying the six classes of tea, with
identification and location photography
throughout"—Provided by publisher.
1. Tea. 2. Tea—Purchasing. 3. Cookery (Tea)
I. Heiss, Robert J. II. Title.
TX415.H438 2010
641.3'372—dc22

                2009038326

ISBN 978-1-58008-804-6

Printed in China

Design by Toni Tajima
Food styling by Bergren Rameson
    and Alexa Hyman
Photography assistance by
    Cody Pickens, Christina
    McNeill, and Ashley French
Photography by Eliot Jordan:
    page 9 (top)
Photography by Saunam
    Bhattacharjee: page 120

10 9 8 7 6 5 4 3 2 1

First Edition

CONTENTS

INTRODUCTION:
The Glorious World of Tea

How times have changed! Premium tea is enjoying the spotlight today in ways unimagined just a few short years ago. Until the 1990s, retail purveyors of premium tea in the United States could be counted on one hand, and specialty food stores stocked just a tame selection of humdrum black tea blends. At best, these selections were marked by country of origin, with perhaps a simple attribution to style of tea or country of production. Unlike today, little detailed information was available to tea drinkers, and most people did not even know what questions to ask. For many, tea was, well, not very exciting, but something that you could count on Grandma to have on hand.

Today, we are learning how enticing and pleasingly distinctive premium tea really is. Tea can be subtle and alluring, bold and bracing, sweet and fresh, young and full of vigor, or rich and matured. It is always fragrant and welcoming at all times. Premium teas once unknown in the West are now becoming familiar, and new tea shops and tea houses are opening for business across the country. For tea enthusiasts, this offers a superb opportunity to travel the world of tea one delicious cup at a time.

Crafting fine tea requires a highly developed sense of perception for touch, sight, and sound that no machine can replicate. And every tea—from Taiwan's Ali Shan High Mountain gao shan oolong to a brisk and bright Ceylon black tea from the Nuwara Eliya region of Sri Lanka—tells a story in the cup about the soil and air that nurtured it and the tea-making skills that transformed and shaped it.

So get ready to explore the world of premium tea, with information to decipher tea lists, tea labels, and tea menus and to purchase a varied selection of wonderful and delicious tea with assurance.

About Our Book

In our thirty-five years as retailers of premium tea, we have been asked just about every possible question regarding tea, tea steeping, and tea storage. We have kept these questions in mind as we approached the topics in our book.

Right up front, let us say that we define *tea* in the classic, historic sense as a caffeinated beverage brewed from the leaf of the *Camellia sinensis* bush. While it is commonplace today to refer to noncaffeinated, herbal beverages such as peppermint, chamomile, and lavender as "tea," we believe that such beverages should be called by other, more appropriate names, such as herbal teas, herbal infusions, or tisanes. Many of these beverages are delicious and refreshing, but they lie outside the scope of our book, and we leave discussion of them to others.

The world's best teas comprise a tiny percentage of the yearly worldwide production of tea. Yet to us, these teas are the most significant. Therefore, our book focuses its attention on pure, unblended, premium teas from the tea-producing countries that have made the greatest contributions to the art and science of tea cultivation and manufacture: China, Japan, India, Sri Lanka, and Taiwan. As a result of learning, observing the results, and perfecting their techniques in the tea factories, generations of tea masters in these countries have created the most stunning teas imaginable.

We believe that learning as much as possible about tea and the process of artisan tea manufacture will heighten your enjoyment of each cup you steep. We hope you take delight in our journey through the vibrant world of tea.

A Simple Cup of Tea Is No Simple Matter

Tea is an essential beverage that quenches the collective thirst of millions of people every day. Whereas tea was once grown only in China, today tea is cultivated in forty-one (and counting!) countries of the world, and new tea industries are developing as worldwide demand increases for more various types of tea.

Tea drinking has never gone out of fashion—it has simply changed course and usage with each new generation of tea drinkers. Tea, the most widely consumed beverage on the planet after water, still proudly maintains its title as the world's oldest beverage. Tea is a wonderfully intricate and complex commodity. There are said to be approximately twenty thousand different distinctions of tea made in the world, a vast number by anybody's count. Yet, no two teas ever taste exactly alike, and every great tea has a distinctive, trademark flavor. You might even say that tea has a cultural identity.

Yet, all tea is made from the fresh leaf of the *Camellia sinensis* bush, and its three major varieties:

- *Camellia sinensis* var. *sinensis* (small-leaf China bush)
- *Camellia sinensis* var. *assamica* (large-leaf Assam bush)
- *Camellia sinensis* var. *cambodi* (medium-leaf Java bush)

Additionally, in parts of Burma (known today as Myanmar), China, India, Laos (officially Lao People's Democratic Republic), Thailand, and Vietnam, strains of indigenous tea bushes and old tea trees coexist with hundreds of local cultivars that have been developed to better meet the needs of tea growers in their specific environments. Since all tea starts as freshly plucked leaf, it is theoretically possible to turn any fresh tea leaf into any of the six classes of tea: green, yellow, white, oolong, black, and Pu-erh.

But tea manufacture is a precise, controlled, and predictable process, and in most tea-producing countries, tea producers focus on only one or two classes of tea. Japan, for instance, produces primarily green teas, but they are very distinctive and taste like no other green teas in Asia. On the other hand, China, the country that unlocked the secrets of tea making and established the manufacturing process for each of the six classes of tea, is the only country that produces all six classes of tea.

What explains the seemingly endless selection of tea available for sale in grocery stores and tea shops? The answer is *terroir*, or place. *Terroir* is the culmination of all the reasons why, for example, Chinese green teas are so different from Japanese green teas. The same forces that work to create all of the wonderful wines and cheese that are so distinctive and appealing are also at work in every tea garden around the world. *Terroir* is not just about the place where a plant grows, but also includes numerous other influences that are responsible for the variation in tea. Let's take a look at all of them.

Terroir: Why Tea Is Unique

This word *terroir* has meaning that can fill volumes. By its most simple definition, *terroir* refers to the place where the roots of a bush or tree or plant nestle into the ground, and the effects that a distinctive environment, including geography, climate, and weather, contributes to the unique character and taste of a food.

However, our visits to tea-producing countries have shown us that other unique particulars also contribute to the overall effects of *terroir* and the distinctive differences among teas. These include the subvariety or cultivar of tea bush (generally, subvarieties are naturally occuring and cultivars are the result of human intervention), cultivation practices, the season of the pluck, the method of leaf manufacture, and the craft of tea making.

Tea that is grown in the high, thin air of the Himalaya in eastern Nepal will invariably taste different than tea that is grown in the low-lying, hot, and humid river valley region of Assam, India. What is it like where the particular tea bushes grow? Do the bushes go dormant over the winter or produce new leaf year-round? Are there weather conditions such as monsoon seasons or frost that affect the leaf and subsequently the taste of the tea?

Terroir can have a large connotation, such as tea from India or tea from China, or it can refer to a small, specific geographic connotation, such as tea from the Huang Shan in Anhui Province, China. *Terroir* distinguishes between locations within the same country as well as between countries.

When we look at all of the tea produced in the regions of any one tea-producing country, we see a composite of teas from north and south, coastal areas, and inland regions. Each *terroir* has specific tea bush cultivars that contribute leaf of a particular character and style to the teas made in that region. When the elements of place are distinctive and strong, they conspire to keep a particular tea from being able to be duplicated in exactly the same way in other places. The sum total of all of the unique places and teas in any one tea-producing country combines to create the collective regional or national character.

Tea Bush Subvarieties and Cultivars

Three main varieties of *Camellia sinensis* (and thousands of subvarieties and cultivars) flourish in tea gardens around the world. It is important that a tea bush variety is planted in a place where that bush will thrive. The foibles of the English in the nineteenth century when they first attempted to cultivate tea in India are a perfect example of what happens when the wrong tea bush variety is chosen for a given location. What many may not realize is that the tea bush variety works with *terroir* to provide the backbone style and to influence the flavor of the tea.

In China, several tea-producing regions in the provinces of Fujian, Guangdong, and Yunnan have native strains of tea bushes and tea trees (some are centuries old) that are not found elsewhere on earth. The fresh leaf from these indigenous varieties is responsible for much of the unique character of the tea from these regions. If you compare tea that is made from old tea tree leaf with one made from the leaf of a modern tea bush cultivar planted nearby, the difference in taste and aroma is quite noticeable.

Tea bush varieties and cultivars look different from one another, too, which means that they act differently during manufacture. Some bushes grow faster or slower; others produce large or small leaves that are thick or thin, less or more serrated on the edges. Tea bush varieties and cultivars have long been overlooked in tea conversations in the West, but this is changing. Many of the nuances of body, fragrance, taste, and aftertaste in tea are influenced by the tea bush variety or cultivar.

Cultivation Practices

Many tea gardens use sustainable farming methods that utilize natural, biodynamic, or organic tea-growing practices. This creates healthier plants by enriching the soil and encouraging the roots of the tea bushes to grow and spread deep into the ground.

To keep the tea bushes healthy and vigorous, ensuring optimal growth and leaf production, and good-tasting tea, workers follow a yearly timetable of scheduled pruning, pest control, fertilizing, and replacing old or damaged tea bushes.

The Season of the Pluck

From the beginning of the tea harvest until the last day of each tea season, millions of tea pluckers fan out into the fields to pluck tender, fresh leaf. Most premium tea is still plucked by hand (with the exception of the mechanical cutters used in Japan and other "modern" tea industries).

In all tea gardens, seasonal changes occur throughout the year. These differences are reflected in the appearance, flavor, and aroma of the tea. The tea-garden manager must set the plucking schedule to accommodate for the rapidly growing tea leaves by the season and the month of the harvest, the weather, and what configuration of fresh leaf needs to be plucked.

Method of Leaf Manufacture

Bringing out desirable tastes and aromas from raw tea leaves requires a delicate balance of creativity; skill; and sound, fresh leaf. The steps of premanufacture, manufacture, and postmanufacture—that which is done to fresh tea leaf after it has been plucked—is the challenge of the tea-factory manager and a team of highly skilled workers.

The tea-factory manager must know the intricacies of the manufacturing process and be able to make adjustments due to weather-related delays, growth spurts in the leaf due to unusually hot weather, and so on. All the effort put into the leaf up to this point can be completely ruined by a misstep during leaf manufacture.

In the simplest terms, leaf manufacture is the process of turning freshly plucked leaf into finished tea. Each class of tea is manufactured according to a well-defined, precise sequence of steps (some manufacture takes longer and is more complicated than others) that is responsible for the differences in green, yellow, white, oolong, black, and Pu-erh tea.

Because the traditional ways of crafting tea differ from region to region, and because humans must work with what nature provides for them on any given day, no two teas will ever be exactly alike. In fact, taking into account all the influences of *terroir*, no two batches of even the "same" tea will ever be exactly alike.

The Craft of Tea Making: History, Culture, and Custom

The learned and skilled contribution of tea workers permeates every aspect of tea: from the tea garden to the tea factory to the tea table. How people do things and why they do them is the rich stuff of culture and tradition that establishes process and practice.

Crafting premium tea requires the senses of a skilled artisan who relies on his or her senses of sight, smell, touch, and hearing to determine how a tea is progressing. Young tea makers learn by observing the older generation of master tea processors make critical adjustments to the leaf during processing that the masters know are needed but perhaps cannot explain in words: hands feeling the leaf as it changes during the stages of manufacture, eyes watching the progress of the leaf as it yields to the heat and begins to hold its final shape, ears listening for the sounds of leaf responding to the heat of the firing pan, and nose detecting the development of aroma in the leaf as it comes closer to becoming tea.

Cultural habits, customs, and the history of a place also influence the teas made there. In many places, tea-making practices are carried out within the boundaries of established traditions. Much is preserved and little is changed: for great-tasting premium tea, this is a very good thing.

A simple cup of tea is no easy matter. Tea is as rich and intricate a subject as wine is for those who choose to explore its many layers. It appeals to our sense of adventure and the exotic; many books have been written about tea's scandalous history and glorious culture. In fact, tea drinking can be a great exercise in armchair travel—all that is required is a trip to a tea shop and a desire to explore the wonderful world of tea in your teacup.

云南普洱茶 名扬

CHAPTER ONE

PURCHASING TEA

What is the best way to determine the merits of a tea, and what are the factors that define this benchmark? Price? Rarity? Grade? Leaf style? Deliciousness? The promise of "High Quality" or the "World's Finest"?

All of these can be a measure used to influence the price of a tea. But cost or rarity alone do not ensure a tasty tea. Beware the oft-used and usually meaningless phrases "high-quality" or "world's finest" which many vendors attach to their tea. This is simply advertising and should be disregarded when evaluating tea. Other, more reliable variables can be counted on to assess a batch of tea.

We prefer to begin judging the potential merits of a tea by evaluating its *soundness*. Soundness is the overall impression that a tea has on us when we look at it. A sound tea consists of tea leaves that are even in color or tone; relatively uniform in shape and size; and pleasant and enticing in aroma. The tea should give the overall impression that it is robust and wholesome, and in prime condition, not faded, lackluster, and past its prime. Condition and appearance, as well as taste, are important in tea.

Chinese tea drinkers evaluate all aspects of tea in three phases:

- Dry leaf, which is evaluated for color and shape
- Tea liquor (the professional tea taster's term for "liquid," sippable tea), which is evaluated for aroma and taste
- Wet leaf after steeping, which is evaluated for shape, color, and aroma

What is being evaluated is how well the tea fits the *expected appearance* (color, leaf size, and shape) and *flavor profile* that it should have. Every Chinese tea has a standard of excellence that the tea maker strives to meet and with which Chinese tea enthusiasts are familiar. For instance, Pan Long Yin Hao, a green tea, should show us that it is made from small, delicate leaves plucked very early in the spring from newly emerging leaves. Pan Long Yin Hao has an expected signature shape and size; if it does not, then something is wrong. Anhui Province's delightful Keemun Mao Feng should be a fairly thin leaf and solid black in color, whereas Yunnan Province's Dian Hong should consist entirely of plump, golden buds.

From the Chinese example, we have expanded our evaluation of tea into six criteria when we are purchasing tea to sell in our store:

- Overall appearance of the leaf
- Aroma of the dry leaf
- Aroma of the liquor
- Color of the liquor
- Aroma and appearance of the wet leaf
- Flavor of the liquor

Learn to Identify and Evaluate Tea

Our desire to know more about where our food and beverages come from and who produces it is, in a sense, putting a place and a face on tea and tea production. If you are new to tea and not sure how to begin, start with a visit to your local tea shop.

A well-stocked tea shop can be an overwhelming place, but the staff is there to help. Tell them what you have in mind: Will the tea be a gift or something for yourself? Perhaps you want to try an oolong tea for the first time, or are looking for a tea that you can drink every morning of the week. Tea shops will help you identify tea and learn the unique qualities of each tea. Before long, you will be able to distinguish one class of tea from another and pinpoint which country made a particular tea.

Begin your tea adventures by setting up a small notebook and keeping it handy whenever you purchase a new tea. If you record information about your purchases, you will be amazed how quickly this information becomes useful as you develop your eye and your palate. Make notes for every tea you try, and add entries for other details that become important to you:

- Name of the tea
- Class of the tea
- Country of production
- Exact grade of the tea
- Where you purchased the tea
- What you like or do not like about the tea
- What other teas it reminds you of: pro or con

TO WHICH CLASS OF TEA DOES THIS TEA BELONG?

The first step in identifying tea is to be able to learn the visual appearances and flavor differences among the six classes of tea: green, yellow, white, oolong, black, and Pu-erh. The teas within each class of tea have a distinctive appearance (and flavor), and it is generally very easy to tell them apart.

OVERALL APPEARANCE OF THE LEAF

Whole-leaf premium tea should have a beautiful, artistic appearance and bear no resemblance to the cut-tear-curl (CTC) or broken leaves used to fill standard tea bags. All tea is graded by size in the tea factory, and premium tea should be comprised of whole leaf that is clean and consistent in size. In order for tea to produce the best flavor when steeped, it must be graded well. If tea has undergone rough handling, and the leaves become crushed before it is sold, the flavor will suffer. Tea that contains discernible amounts of stems or other bits of foreign matter, broken leaf, or accumulated bits of tea dust is not premium tea and should not be purchased.

Tea should have a clean, sound look that suggests it was properly manufactured and handled. Unless the tea is a blend, the leaf should be recognizable by appearance and be consistent with the style of the tea. Most tea can be identified by the shape and color of the leaves. If tea has a dull, lackluster appearance, pass on it.

For example, Wu Yi Shan rock oolong tea leaves should be long and leafy, thick and plump, and slightly rumpled or twisted and smoky gray-black in color; they are never small and choppy.

For all tea, the overall color and tone of the leaf should be consistent within the batch. For example, some tea has a lot of tip, others some tip, and many types have no tip. No matter how much tip there is, the leaf should be uniform in size and appearance. With a few exceptions (sheng Pu-erh, Bai Hao Taiwan oolong, and the leafy white teas from Fujian, China), leaf color should not be a mixture of tones, thicknesses, and lengths.

Sound tea will have an even finish; the leaf should not be streaky or have blister spots (which indicates that the fresh leaf came in contact with a surface that was too hot). Poorly made or old tea will have a dull, faded appearance.

AROMA OF THE DRY LEAF

All tea has aroma, but the aroma of some leaf is delicate, and more pronounced in others. A subtle fragrance should not be mistaken for faded aroma or old tea, and a strong aroma does not indicate better tea.

Good aroma should reflect the natural plant origins of tea and not smell like cardboard or plastic, or the peppercorns that someone placed next to the bag of tea. It is also important to differentiate between natural tea aroma and highly aromatized teas, such as jasmine, Lapsang Souchong, mango-apricot, or orange-spiced tea. The aroma of these teas has been created either during the manufacturing process (natural or artificial flower blossom scenting for jasmine tea and cold or hot wood-smoking for Lapsang Souchong) or by the addition of flavorings and spices (such as cinnamon, ginger, orange peel, and so on) after manufacture.

AROMA OF THE LIQUOR

Tea has complex and evocative aromas that can make one want to drink a cup *immediately*. Good tea aroma should bring to mind enticing elements from the natural environment of the tea garden or from the charcoal-firing steps of tea manufacture: plant greenery, bamboo, wood, mushrooms, flowers, grass, snow, nuts, spices, wood charcoal, and more.

COLOR OF THE LIQUOR

Sound tea should have clarity and sparkle in the cup. Who wants to sip a cup of murky tea? The color of tea liquor in the cup should be appropriate to the manufacture. Some black teas are deep red in the cup, while others are cherry-red, but all black teas should fall into the red/brown/orange color wheel. Some Chinese white teas are pale green, others yellow-green. So, if your rare pre-Qing Ming China green tea looks vaguely like your aged sheng Pu-erh, there is a problem.

AROMA AND APPEARANCE OF THE WET LEAF

Leaf tea in its rehydrated state is the closest it will ever be to its original, fresh state. The aroma of the wet leaf should be indicative of the flavor of the liquor that will follow; in general, it should have the engaging smell of leafy plant matter or wet greens. There should be no off-putting smell or previously undetected unpleasant odor.

FLAVOR OF THE LIQUOR

This is the final test, and the culmination of all of the work in the tea gardens and tea factories. There are many nuances of taste and flavor expressed in tea that can never be fully described or tamed; they must be experienced with the senses. Every day that tea is made in a tea factory it will taste a tiny bit different than the same tea that was made the day before. This might be because the leaf is a micrometer larger, or because the weather required a slight adjustment to the manufacture, or simply because the beauty of handmade tea is that each batch can never be precisely the same.

Tea should have a distinctive flavor that identifies it as what it is (ah yes, a Wu Yi Shan oolong), even if it is a Wu Yi Shan oolong that you have not tasted before. The taste should hit the right note of complexity and depth, high oxidation and roasting, and possess background hints of spice, fruit, or a general "floral" quality. It should not be sour, thin, or watery or overly astringent or woody.

The flavor is the culmination of all that attracted you to a particular batch of tea in the first place; it should be a good example of its type and not disappoint. But when you are disappointed (and when you can rule out with certainty that improper measuring, water at the wrong temperature, or careless steeping were not the cause), there is a lesson to learn from that experience as well. It is not possible to love every tea one tastes, but there is as much to learn from tasting tea that you don't like as there is from tea that you do like. Trial and error, taste, taste, taste . . . it's all part of being a tea enthusiast!

Single-Garden Estate Tea versus Blended Tea

This topic elicits strong opinions from tea drinkers. Estate specificity offers the tea enthusiast myriad distinctive flavor components and complexity, while blended tea offers easy drinking and a balanced flavor profile. Choosing the best tea one can afford to drink and understanding the differences that both choices have to offer is what is important.

SINGLE-GARDEN ESTATE TEA

Single-garden estate teas are unblended teas grown on a specific tea estate or tea garden. The name of a tea garden located within a region of any tea-producing country is the equivalent of an address: it is an actual place where the tea bushes that the particular tea was plucked from are located. This indicator is also called a "garden mark." For example, tea that is marked "Jungpana Estate SFTGFOP 1, 2008 1st

Flush, Darjeeling, India," gives us the name of the estate and the grade of the tea, the year and season of the pluck (first flush is spring), and the region and country of origin.

Estate teas offer tea enthusiasts the best examples of the extraordinary diversity of flavor that premium tea has to offer. These teas reflect what the effects of *terroir* have conspired to bring to the taste of the leaf in any given season. If the weather before or during the harvest season is uncooperative, the tea harvest may result in a disappointing tea for that season. Nevertheless, estate teas are always sold unblended but graded.

Indian, Sri Lankan, African, and Indonesian teas are labeled in a similar fashion. In China the name of the tea and the region and province is given, but often not the grade. It is becoming more common to see a year and season attributed to the tea, so a label might read "2009 pre-Qing Ming Longjing, Meijiawu Village, Xihu District, Hangzhou City, Zhejiang Province, China." In Japan tea is sold by type of tea: for example, Sencha, along with the prefecture, region, village, or famous tea-growing area. An example might be "Gyokuro, Uji, Kyoto prefecture, Japan."

BLENDED TEA

Blended teas are those teas that are a combination of teas from different regions or countries. Irish Breakfast and English Breakfast are two very popular tea blends. Most blends rely on upwards of six to eight different teas sourced from different countries to yield the familiar flavor that the tea packer and their customers seek. When skillfully and intentionally combined, such blends are delicious, and the taste remains constant from batch to batch.

Tea blenders attempt to keep the flavor profile of their blended tea consistent at all times; they do this by carefully harmonizing the selection of teas that comprise the blend. Teas are substituted as necessary, and it is the job of a good tea blender to keep these changes as seamless as possible in the final taste of the tea.

New Tea versus Aged Tea

Experienced tea enthusiasts know that there is goodness in both new tea and aged tea. Each offers a different taste and tea-drinking experience, yet both are part of the "yin and yang" that contribute to the complexity and wonder of tea.

NEW TEA: THE BLUSH OF YOUTH

In countries where tea bushes rest during a period of winter dormancy, tea that is plucked during the weeks when winter is retreating under the advance of early spring is especially prized. Tea pluckers race against the clock to gather the smallest buds and leaves from tea bushes that are flushing with new growth. Workers in the tea factories work equally fast to process these first-of-the-season tender leaves into fine, flavorsome tea and ship them quickly to market where tea lovers eagerly await their annual return.

China produces a small but select listing of green, yellow, and black pre-Qing Ming teas (those plucked before April 5) each year that are delightfully refreshing. For Darjeeling tea enthusiasts, the arrival of aromatic and youthful first-flush (February/March) teas are eagerly awaited. In Japan, the earliest teas are plucked in a ten-day to two-week period beginning in early April and are known as Shincha. In Taiwan, the most sought after of the famous High Mountain gao shan teas are the sweet winter teas that are plucked in December. The air is cold and the leaves grow at a slower rate, yielding tea with concentrated flavors, reduced tannins, and beguiling stony, floral aromas.

All of these teas are more expensive than teas that come to market later as the season progresses. But for tea enthusiasts these new teas provide the opportunity to experience superbly aromatic, fresh, dynamic tastes that reflect a brief moment in time in the harvest cycle. Look for the arrival of new-season tea in the United States beginning at the end of April each year. Be sure to drink these teas within the year; their youthful vigor does not keep.

AGED TEA: RICHNESS AND FINESSE

Not all tea is capable of aging, but some oolongs, black, and Pu-erh teas can age magnificently. Anyone who has experienced the wonderful flavors of fine red wines, and vintage spirits such as brandy or Calvados, understands that certain magical "something" that the effects of maturation exert on flavor, body, mouthfeel, and aroma.

Unfortunately, it is costly to allow products to age before bringing them to market. Asian and Southeast Asian tea enthusiasts often buy tea with the intention of aging it at home. The aromas of aged tea are mellow and rounded, and the flavors have deepened into something rich and expansive. The older the tea is that you serve to your guests, the more honor you bestow on them.

Aged teas are prized for the increased energy (*cha-qi*) that they possess, and for their ability to connect with and increase the level of internal bodily energy (*qi*) in those sipping these teas. This marriage of *cha-qi* and *qi* generates strong feelings of contentment and peacefulness within the tea drinker and is an anticipated and esteemed trait that is especially powerful and prevalent in aged teas. *Cha-qi* is present in teas that have been grown organically in an environment that has not been polluted with chemicals, either now or in the past. Aging can increase the amount and intensity of *cha-qi* but is not the sole reason for its presence.

Examples of Tea-Package Labeling

Varying amounts of information will be offered on a tea label, from detailed to minimal information. A single-garden estate tea may include information on the type of tea, year and season of harvest, and origin of tea (country, district or province, estate, and garden). Other details may be included on a tea label (and are used by some countries but not others), such as the tea bush cultivar, firing style, oxidation level, or level of roasting. Some famous teas are protected from labeling and packing abuse and display a seal or logo that authenticates the tea, such as the Darjeeling tea logo. Other tea packages may be marked that the tea contained inside is 100 percent from the said place of origin. Additionally, if the tea has a value-added incentive, such as an organic certification or is connected to a social justice program such as Fair Trade, then the package will display the appropriate seals of those organizations as well.

Grades of Tea

All tea is graded by the size or shape of the finished leaf after manufacture. Green, yellow, white, and scented teas are graded on different criteria than black, oolong, or Pu-erh teas, and the terminology used by each tea-producing country, while based on the same criteria, will vary. Refer to chapter three for more detailed information about grading for each class of tea.

Where to Purchase Tea

Different retailers sell different types of tea, so knowing where to look for what you want to purchase will save you time and money. The obvious places to purchase tea are supermarkets, specialty food stores, tea shops and tea houses, and Internet vendors.

SUPERMARKETS

Assuredly, supermarkets are not the places to look for premium tea. The emphasis there is on everyday tea, and the operative words are inexpensive and undistinguished. In the tea aisle, tea bags are king, and the selection, while representing many different companies, is, when you break down which teas are commonly used to fill the tea bags, really comprised of only a few choices.

Once the domain of black tea, green tea now accounts for quite a bit of shelf space in supermarkets. The emphasis is, sadly, on green tea that is hyped up with additional antioxidants, vitamins, and flavoring, and not on the quality or flavor of the tea.

SPECIALTY FOOD STORES

Specialty food stores stock branded, packaged teas that range from just a cut above what one finds in the supermarket to tea brands that are very good. But if you are a real tea enthusiast, you will rarely find the tea of your dreams. Some of these brands offer blended black tea, such as English Breakfast tea, but more commonly their offerings are slanted toward flavored, scented, or spiced teas that are proprietary. Specialty tea brands are beginning to offer a more even split between tea bags and loose-leaf tea, and a few brands offer selections of pure leaf tea from individual tea-producing countries.

TEA SHOPS AND TEA HOUSES

These are the places to find the best and most interesting selections of premium, pure, orthodox leaf tea. Some tea shops package their tea selections under their own label, while others weigh tea to order for their customers. Either way, tea shops have control over the teas that they choose to sell, and thus customers gain control as well. Here, you can purchase exactly the tea you want, and you can often look at the tea as well.

It is important that you shop for tea where:

- The teas are fresh and they turn over frequently.
- Each of the teas has been selected for a reason (not just because a salesperson told the tea merchant that it is a popular seller).
- A good cross-section of green, white, oolong, and black teas are available.

Like all well-run independent specialty shops, a reputable tea shop exudes a discernable passion and enthusiasm for its tea. These shops care how fresh their tea is, where their tea comes from, and how it is made. The attitude of the shop owner and staff is conveyed not only in the selection of teas offered, but also in how they treat and handle the tea and whether or not the staff engage customers in conversation about tea and share educational bits of information with them. If it is apparent that the shop is only interested in making a sale and not educating customers, shop elsewhere. Ditto if the salespeople are not knowledgeable or if they are unwelcoming.

Tea merchants who have the opportunity to visit a tea-producing country might return with or have some small

quantities of tea shipped to them from tea producers abroad. This is wonderful for tea enthusiast customers, but it is not necessary that tea merchants purchase from the source in order to sell exceptional tea. Direct trade can be complicated, and without a basis of trust and the goodwill necessary for a mutually advantageous situation, there is an equal chance that the tea ordered will not be the tea sent. Tea merchants have more to gain by establishing a trusted relationship with established tea importers (who provide a valuable service in handling all of the difficult work and headaches of importing) than they do trying to go it alone.

The Importance of Trust and Relationships

In the West, we are often not able to taste tea before we purchase it. That's okay, but it is important that you at least see the tea, because quality assessment can be made from visual clues. Sniffing the aroma of the dry leaf will not tell you how the tea will taste, but aroma is a good indicator of overall freshness and whether the tea is scented or smoked, or has picked up an "off" odor.

When you are not able to see the tea (when ordering online or when the tea is sold in a sealed package), then you will have to make a judgment based on the experience you have had with that vendor or tea brand. If you are purchasing from a tea merchant whose judgment and integrity regarding soundness and freshness you trust, and who has proven to have a good palate and a discerning eye for good tea, then you can feel confident that all of the teas are chosen as carefully as the teas you have previously experienced. If a tea shop specializes in a certain style of tea—say, green teas or oolongs—then this may be a bias, and the rest of the teas may not be as good.

If the merchant is someone with whom you have no experience, purchase a small amount of several teas to become familiar with the offerings. What ultimately matters when purchasing tea is that you expect to trust the vendor and that the vendor then earns that trust by selling you sound, well-chosen tea.

INTERNET TEA STORES

We all know that the Internet is a wild card—a place filled with as many great opportunities as it has scams and nefarious individuals. An impressive amount of tea is offered for sale over the Internet.

Some of this tea is sold by brick-and-mortar stores who also maintain a cyber presence. Other "storefronts" operate only on the Internet; some are tea companies, others are individuals selling tea as a side business, and some are venture capitalists seizing opportunity.

One of the key ways to evaluate a site is to look at what they tell you about themselves, who they are, where they are, and the depth of the information they present about the tea they are selling. When no information can be gleaned about who is behind the website or where they are physically located, we shop elsewhere, because the likelihood is small that this site will be selling premium tea. Word of mouth is a great indicator—check with your friends to see which tea vendors they like.

"Same" Tea, Different Prices—Which to Choose?

When you come across two teas with the "same" name but two different prices, do not assume they are the same tea.

Not all tea is created equal, and most teas are sold in many grades and from several seasons. For instance, two different vendors may both have a tea that is sold under the same name (and that appears to be the same tea), but it does not mean the two teas are the same in grade or soundness. One tea merchant may have a premium version of that tea, while the other may be selling something that is seriously disappointing. Your ability to evaluate the tea and the situation will pay off. Shopping by price alone does not guarantee value or the finest tea.

CHAPTER TWO

STEEPING THE PERFECT CUP

Fresh leaf is plucked in an instant, with a snap of the wrist, from bushes pulsing with the renewed energy of seasonal rebirth and growth. Under the watchful gaze of a tea artisan, this leaf is rolled, shaped, and dried with care, sealing in the flavor and aroma for release in the cup. Skillful steeping unlocks the delicious attributes of these leaves.

Steeping a pot of tea is about intuitively knowing the best way to steep a particular leaf, and how the resulting tea should taste. Chinese tea masters refer to water as a friend to tea: water heated to the right temperature for a tea will yield a cup that reveals the subtle flavors and character of that tea. Too little or too much heat and the flavor will be suppressed or ruined. By paying attention to your tea and its ideal steeping conditions, you can learn to avoid the three most common mistakes of tea steeping:

- Using too much or not enough tea
- Improper water temperature
- Oversteeping

The Chemistry of a Cup of Tea

In terms of chemistry, a cup of tea is a color-tinged aqueous liquid composed of many water-soluble components that dissipate from the dry leaf on contact with heated water. The most important water-soluble components (those that dissolve in water and will be present in your cup of tea versus other components of tea that are not in your cup because they are water-insoluble) are listed here, not only for their contributions to the tactile sensation of tea liquor but also because careful attention paid to the steps of tea steeping will keep these components in balance, resulting in a tasty cup of tea as opposed to one that is not worth a second sip.

AMINO ACIDS

Tea contains nearly two dozen amino acids, the most important of which is *theanine*, responsible for transmitting the flavor of tea. Theanine also contributes the calming effect that drinking a cup of tea has been proven to have by minimizing the effects of caffeine. The presence of theanine is the primary reason why drinking several cups of tea does not bring on the caffeine jag that drinking several cups of coffee does for most people.

TANNINS

Tea contains flavanols (the tea catechins) that are responsible for the healthful, antioxidant benefits of tea (different beneficial antioxidant compounds exist in oxidized versus nonoxidized tea) and the texture of tea liquor. Three of the flavanols—kaempferol, myricetin, and quercetin—add astringency.

ALKALOIDS

Caffeine, along with theophylline and theobromine, represent the trinity of alkaloids that give tea its stimulating qualities. In premium tea, this component contributes a pleasant bite; in low-quality tea, it adds sheer bitterness.

VOLATILE COMPOUNDS

A variety of volatile compounds are responsible for banding together and creating the elusive, beguiling, tantalizing, and sometimes hard-to-put-your-finger-on aroma of tea liquor.

VITAMINS AND MINERALS

Although tea leaves also contain beta-carotene (which is converted in the liver to vitamin A) and vitamin E (water-insoluble), it is the water-soluble vitamins B2 (riboflavin) and C that are ingestible in your cup of tea and contribute to the healthful benefits of drinking tea.

a wandering mind spoils the tea—
awareness and well-made tea are one and the same

Making Peace with Your Tea: Eastern and Western Differences in Steeping Tea

In Asia, the process of tea leaves unfurling in a cup of heated water is referred to as "the breathing and stretching of the leaves." In the West, the same process has been called "the agony of the leaves." These phrases conjure up two very different images for the same action: the hydration of tea leaves as they slowly become saturated with water and release their flavor into the cup. The first image implies a careful, tranquil, and positive process; the second, a stressful and anguished activity. The former invokes images of a delicate green or white tea; the latter, a robust black tea. While each may be an expression of a culture's thoughts regarding the process of steeping tea, these images present an ideal opportunity to address the conceptual aspects of preparing tea.

In the West, we drink our tea differently than people do in Asian cultures. We add milk and sugar to our tea; we often eat food or sugary sweets with our tea; and we steep copious amounts of tea in large teapots. The most common sizes for English teapots are six cups (thirty-six ounces) or eight cups (forty-eight ounces); in Asia, teapots are often designed to steep six ounces of tea or less. The need to drink a quantity of tea from a large cup or mug is strictly a Western habit. Large cups require more tea to fill them, and that means bigger teapots.

Historically, tea-producing countries developed and manufactured tea for their own consumption. They also developed unique teapots and methods of steeping their teas that extracted the best flavor from the tea leaves and suited their taste preferences. The tea industries in Ceylon, India, and Indonesia were started by the British and the Dutch for the purpose of manufacturing black tea for export to the European and American markets. Because of this, the style and flavor of black teas were designed to suit Western preferences regarding flavor, steeping methods, serving, and drinking habits.

Understanding different teas and their steeping requirements will result in better-tasting tea than steeping every tea "Western style" will. Different methods used with the same tea leaves can result in very different infusions. Some of these will be successful, others not. Knowing how to steep each class of tea is similar to (but not any more difficult than) knowing which wines are best served chilled and which ones are not.

Wherever you find yourself in the world of tea drinking, there will be customs and mores that dictate the procedures used to prepare the tea being enjoyed. Whether English-style black tea with dairy and scones, Russian-style tea sweetened with jam, or East Asian tea served with hard-boiled quail eggs and a bowl of peanuts, the cultural aspects of tea drinking contribute greatly to the enjoyment of the occasion.

For Asian tea drinkers, there is an expectation on the part of the host who prepares the tea and the tea drinkers who share it regarding the tea and the common experience of drinking tea together. The experience is all about the tea; the preparation, steeping, and drinking utilize all five senses.

- **Look.** Look at, appreciate, and evaluate the unique appearance, shape, and color of the leaf.
- **Touch.** Feel the dry tea leaves. Are they light or soft, dense or fluffy? Feel the clay and the glaze of the tea cup: is it smooth or rough?
- **Hear.** Listen to the sound of the water simmering in the kettle and then as it is poured into the teapot, the sound of the teapot lid slid across the top of the teapot, and the sound of the tea being poured into the cup.
- **Smell.** Inhale the aroma of both the tea liquor and the wet tea leaves after steeping. Each should have a refreshing and enticing aroma.

- **Taste.** The tea should be a well-balanced combination of sweet, spicy, bitter, and earthy. Each class of tea offers tea enthusiasts something different to savor: from sweet and light to spicy and strong, or with nuances, such as woodsy, floral, kelpy, minerally, and nutty, the overall style and flavor is experienced by the palate as something unique.

Chinese tea drinkers taste tea in three stages (or "three mouths"):

- The tip of the tongue tastes sweetness.
- The middle of the tongue senses tartness.
- The back of the tongue perceives bitterness.

When you really want to taste your tea, use this technique that we learned from one of our Taiwan tea associates.

1. Breathe out.
2. Take a sip.
3. Hold the tea liquor in your mouth and breathe in through your nose.
4. Swallow the tea.
5. Breathe out.
6. The aroma of the tea should fill your retro-nasal passages.

Making a Great-Tasting Cup of Tea

Because whole-leaf tea is manufactured in six classes and in many diverse styles, shapes, and leaf sizes, it is difficult to quote a "one-size-fits-all" measurement for tea. Steeping times will vary with the tea; not all teas (even those with the same name) will respond quite the same way because tea manufactured during a certain season of the year will differ from the "same" tea made in another season. Our suggestion is to try our parameters and then adjust for your tea and your preference.

ASIAN-STYLE STEEPING (MULTIPLE STEEPINGS)

Small unglazed clay teapots or porcelain *gaiwans* (thin-walled, porcelain tea-drinking cups comprised of three pieces—a lid, the cup, and a saucer) are the vessels of choice in China for steeping all classes of tea. Likewise, Japanese, Korean, and Taiwanese tea drinkers use small unglazed clay or ceramic teapots for steeping green, oolong, and Pu-erh teas. The average capacity of these teapots is four to six ounces, but pots can hold as little as two ounces or as much as ten ounces. The tea liquor is always decanted from the teapot directly into teacups or into a small pitcher and never left to sit in the teapot. Tea is always drunk plain.

Small-size teapots allow tea enthusiasts to enjoy multiple steepings of the tea, using short infusions of less than one minute to just over one minute. In order for this process to work correctly, the measurements must be in opposition to those used to steep Western-style tea. Essentially, the teapot or *gaiwan* is filled to approximately one-fourth to one-half capacity with tea and the remainder of the space is filled with water. During each steeping, the water penetrates into the leaf a little more until eventually the water reaches the core of the leaf. Each infusion presents another nuance of flavor, giving the tea drinker slightly different variations in flavor to savor over the course of several infusions.

WESTERN-STYLE STEEPING (SINGLE STEEPING)

The tea in question is usually black tea, which is steeped for three to five minutes, allowing the water to penetrate into the core of the leaf, thereby breaking down the flavor components and extracting all the flavorful goodness from the leaf in one steeping. Western-style teapots often hold more tea than will be consumed in the first serving. Therefore, the tea liquor must be decanted from the teapot or the tea leaves must be removed from the teapot to avoid oversteeping.

USEFUL WAYS TO STEEP
GREAT-TASTING TEA

Understandably, loose-leaf tea initially may seem to lack the convenience of tea bags, but tea enthusiasts know that in addition to being the key to enjoying premium teas, loose-leaf tea has the benefit of being a more ecologically sound method of tea steeping (no individual tea bag envelopes, bags, and strings or extra packaging to toss away).

Ban the Tea Ball

Long ago we banned metal tea balls in our store. Those old-fashioned tea-steeping devices (the ones that screw together or have a squeeze handle) date from a time when nearly all tea drunk in the West was fine-cut black tea generically labeled as "orange pekoe." One teaspoon of that tea was the standard measure per cup. The conventional expected yield from a pound of tea was two hundred cups when measured full-strength. The leaf was measured into a teapot or packed into a tea ball and steeped for five minutes or longer. Milk and sugar could be counted on to take care of any rough edges.

Happily, tea is available today in all manner of shapes, lengths, densities, and sizes. For tea enthusiasts it is unthinkable to damage premium whole-leaf tea by stuffing it into these outdated, small metal tea balls. There are better alternatives.

- **Single-cup mesh filters.** There are inexpensive and easy-to-use stainless steel, gold mesh, and nylon infusers designed to fit into some small teapots or right into one's favorite teacup or mug. These are deep and roomy enough to comfortably hold the largest leaf teas without damaging them; the leaf floats loosely in the infuser, yielding a better-tasting cup of tea. They are ecological and allow the user to steep loose-leaf tea easily.

- **Fill your own paper tea sacks.** A very convenient choice, these variously sized paper pouches made from tea bag paper allow you to use your own loose-leaf tea. At last, this is a way to have the convenience of tea bags together with the size needed to accommodate the needs of whole-leaf tea: greater water circulation and room for the expansion of rehydrating leaf.

Tips for Coaxing the Best Flavor from Your Tea

The goal in steeping tea is to *coax* the flavor from your leaves, not *wrench* it out. Steeping a great-tasting cup of tea is easy. The only requirement is paying attention to a few simple steps in order to find "flavor nirvana" in your cup.

These tea-steeping tips are the mantra of all reliable tea vendors because they are important. And they work.

1. **Measure the leaf.** Use the right amount of leaf—don't guess. Guessing leads to too much or too little leaf in the pot, and this never tastes right. With all the glorious whole-leaf and bud teas available, it is important to evaluate the amount of tea to use each time you encounter a new tea. Adjust the measure of leaf depending on the class of tea and the method that was used to manufacture the tea.

2. **Pay attention to water quality.** Use pure, clean water. Water with too many minerals will affect the taste of the tea, as will municipal tap water that has been treated with chlorine.

3. **Use the correct water temperature.** One of the most important aspects of balancing the water-soluble components in your steeped tea is the temperature of the water you use. If the water temperature is too high, the tea will taste bitter because more of the tannins will be released into the cup. Also, delicate aroma compounds will be driven off and lost. If the temperature is too

low, proper extraction cannot occur, and the tea will taste flat.

4. **Watch your steeping time.** Follow the recommended steeping time for your tea to release only the desireable flavor components. Setting a kitchen timer is a useful practice.

5. **Consider the tea-steeping vessel.** While black, yellow, white, and most green teas will steep well in a Western-style teapot, oolongs, Pu-erh, and some Japanese green teas will perform better in a *gaiwan*—a small unglazed clay teapot. There is a synergy between the ratio of tea and water to the size of the brewing vessel that yields the tastiest cup; take a lead from how tea drinkers in tea-producing countries drink their tea.

Measuring the Leaf: By Weight or Volume

The easiest way to measure leaf tea is to weigh it on a small inexpensive kitchen scale that is calibrated in grams. The ideal ratio of leaf to water for most tea is **two to three grams of tea leaf for six ounces of water.**

For many tea enthusiasts, and in keeping with the natural aesthetic of tea, it is ultimately most satisfying to look at the tea and determine by eye and touch the amount of leaf to use for a cup or a pot of tea. (Familiarity leads to surety, which is the goal of measuring tea. This is not the same as random guessing.) Volume is easy to learn; just keep in mind that **the recommended volume of leaf will vary with the type of tea that you are using.**

Measuring guidelines should take the following variables into consideration:

- **Class** of tea
- **Size** (some leaf is large, other leaf is small)
- **Shape** (rolled leaf vs. straight leaf vs. twisted leaf)
- **Density** (thickness of the leaf)

Leaf size relates to volume, and it is the volume of leaf that is the first important matter. As an example, think a pound of feathers, a pound of nails. Each product weighs one pound, but a bag of feathers is substantially bulkier in volume than a bag of nails. Similarly,

- the larger the leaves, the bulkier they are in volume;
- the smaller and denser the leaves, the more compact they are in volume.

Bulky teas require that you use a greater volume of leaf per six-ounce serving than a small, denser leaf. Let's compare different styles of Assam black teas: (1) a large-leaf orthodox-style tea, and (2) a finely cut orthodox or a CTC ("cut-tear-curl") tea. The latter will steep to a very tasty cup using the standard measure of one teaspoon tea to six ounces of water, but the large-leaf Assam will taste thin if we only use one teaspoon of its leaf. For the large-leaf Assam to taste as it should, we need to triple the volume of leaf per cup. Remember, in tripling the volume of leaf you are not making the steeped tea three times as strong, you are simply increasing the volume of dry leaf used, which keeps it consistent with the weight of the denser Assam tea: both should be two to three grams by weight.

Approximation by volume will be reliable most times. From this baseline, you can begin to fine-tune the quantity of leaf to use for different teas. Following is a table of equivalents for determining quantity of tea by volume measure as well as by weight. (See page 173 for more information on the volume to weight difference of tea leaf.)

MEASURING TEA BY WEIGHT AND VOLUME		
Style of Tea	**Weight**	**Volume**
CTC, small leaf, semiball-rolled tea, small bud tea	2 to 3 grams	1 to 2 teaspoons
Medium-size leaf, medium-size bud tea	2 to 3 grams	2 to 3 teaspoons
Large leaf	2 to 3 grams	1 to 2 tablespoons

Water Quality

A cup of tea is composed of 99 percent water. If the leaf is the soul of a good cup of tea, then water is the heart. It bears constant repetition that the water that you use for making tea must be as pure and delicious as that which you drink from a glass.

It is hard to think of something as natural as water being "bad," but unfortunately, much of our tap water is treated municipally, leaving it safe to drink but bland, stripped of every nuance of flavor it had, or fouled with a chemical taste and a bad odor. Well water can be too hard and too full of minerals. Imported waters can be too soft or too hard.

The best water is fresh, oxygenated, and somewhat sweet tasting. If you must purchase water for tea, experiment with different brands of bottled spring water. The ideal is water with a neutral pH value of 7 (or one that is slightly acidic). Never use distilled water. The small added cost for pure water is worth it; nothing will taint your tea more than bad water. Installing a simple water filter in the home will often result in good water for tea making.

One last caveat: water should be boiled only once. Heating water and regulating the heat to maintain a constant level for a short tea-steeping session is fine; reheating water that has come to a boil and cooled completely will create flat-tasting, lifeless water.

Water Temperature

There is no "one temperature fits all" rule for steeping tea. Water temperature is critical; water that is too hot can scorch the leaves, turning what would have been a nice cup of tea into a bitter stew. It will also rob the tea of its aromatics, rendering the fragrance flat and dull. All the careful handling in the tea gardens and tea factories will be for naught if the water temperature is out of kilter for the intended tea.

Water temperature can be determined visually by watching the change in the motion of the water and the bubbles that form as the water heats. Or you can plunge an instant-read thermometer into the water to gauge the temperature. If you find that the water temperature is too high, move the kettle to a cool burner, open or remove the lid, and let the water cool for a few minutes to the correct temperature before using. Another trick is to add a small quantity of cold water to the hot to bring the water temperature down quickly. (Only do this with water that is pure enough for drinking.) Again, there is some leeway with these temperatures, but try these first, then experiment wisely.

WATER TEMPERATURE FOR STEEPING TEA, BY TYPE	
Tea Type	**Temperature**
White tea, Japanese green tea, and Chinese spring green tea	160° to 170°F. Bring the water to a boil and allow it to rest for 5 minutes before using.
Green tea (standard) Yellow tea	170° to 180°F "Column of Steam Steadily Rising." This is the period during which a visible pillar of steam materializes. Or bring water to a boil and allow it to rest for 3 minutes before using.
Oolong tea	180° to 200°F "Fish Eyes." This is when large lazy bubbles gently break the surface. Or bring water to a boil and allow it to rest for 2 minutes before using.
Black tea	190° to 200°F "String of Pearls." This is the moment almost at the boil, when tiny bubbles appear to loop near the perimeter of the kettle. Or bring the water to a boil and allow it to rest for 1 minute before using.
Pu-erh tea	200° to 212°F "Turbulent Waters." This is a full, rolling boil, when the water is most active. Bring the water to a boil and use it at the boil.

Steeping Time

Steep each new tea with our recommendations, then vary the steeping time to suit your taste preferences. Experiment wisely. Remember, you are coaxing flavor out of delicate tea leaves; work with the tea, not against it.

When tasting a tea that is new to you, start with a two-minute steep, taste it, and taste it again every thirty seconds. Jot down the results. Green, yellow, and white teas are rarely left in the water for longer than two minutes (and often less). Oolong teas can steep from one to five minutes, depending on whether the leaf is a semiball-rolled style or a long, strip-style leaf, and whether the tea is being steeped Asian or Western style. Green, yellow, white, and oolong teas can always be steeped again, at least once but sometimes three times or more, depending on the tea. Additional steepings may call for a cooler or hotter water temperature than that used for the initial steeping. Steeping times for black tea vary depending on the cut of the leaf. Finely cut orthodox leaf and CTC styles usually need just two to three minutes, whereas large-leaf orthodox black teas may need five minutes to fully develop. For information on steeping Pu-erh, and expanded information on all classes of tea, see the detailed instructions in chapter three.

If you follow the above recommendations while you become familiar with the various classes of tea, you will soon be on your way to developing the ability to confidently judge steeping time for your various teas. Here are some tips to keep in mind:

- Always cover your tea when steeping; the tea leaves will unfurl more uniformly and the finished tea will taste better if the teapot or *gaiwan* has been covered.
- Do not wander away from your tea while it is steeping; steeping time ranges from just two to five minutes.

Fill your teacups only two-thirds full; leave the remaining space to collect the feelings and emotions of those who have gathered to drink tea with you.

CHAPTER THREE

THE SIX CLASSES OF TEA

Each of the six classes of tea contributes remarkable-tasting and distinctive-looking teas to the world's bounty. We savor the flavor of delicious tea, but we also delight in looking at the leaves of beautiful, well-made tea. To us, the colors, textures, leaf shapes, and sizes of premium teas are a testament to the skills of artisan tea makers. Some classes of tea, such as black tea, are comprised of thousands of teas from both large and small black tea–producing countries. Other classes, such as white and yellow tea, consist of only a few important teas produced in specific locations. Despite the seemingly endless choices of tea for sale, learning to categorize tea by class of manufacture is easy, and a handy way to begin making sense of the possibilities.

In the West, tea for sale has primarily been black tea from India and Sri Lanka, and basic oolong from Taiwan. These teas were given familiar English names and the emphasis was on country of origin without much further detail. Today, a wealth of tea from China, Japan, and Korea is available, and at first the attempt was made to sell them similarly by country with simple English names. But as tea enthusiasts became more inquiring about origin and the available teas became more numerous, the original Chinese, Japanese, and Korean names of the teas started to appear in transliterated form. Similarly, most English named teas now appear with more regional detail.

In our book we use the most specific current name for each tea. In some cases this includes both the transliterated original name and an English name. Thus, each tea is listed alphabetically in its "Gallery of Teas" by the name that should make it easiest to locate in most premium tea shops. For each class of tea, a map highlights the primary tea-growing regions discussed for that type of tea.

GREEN TEA

Green tea is tea in its purest form and the one that is minimally altered by man. There is no room in green tea production for overmanipulation or drawn-out, fussy techniques. The most critical factors in the manufacture of green tea are preventing oxidation of the fresh leaf and preserving the natural green color.

Green tea offers many different leaf styles and singular flavor characteristics. In the cup, a sip of green tea can be reminiscent of honey, a lightly salty sea spray, a gentle breeze passing through a stand of pines, or pure water washed over stones in a stream. These transitory tastes are accompanied by sweet-smelling aromas that are refreshing, delicious, and uncomplicated.

Green tea is produced year-round in subtropical locations but only at specific times in the warm months in temperate zones. This corresponds to the specific varieties of *Camellia sinensis* grown in these dissimilar places. The quality of the leaf generally relates to the number of plucks (harvests) per year and the time of year in which the pluck occurs.

In regions of the world in which the tropical subvarieties of *Camellia sinensis*, such as Assam bush (*Camellia sinensis* var. *assamica*) or Java bush (*Camellia sinensis* var. *cambodi*), grow, leaf for green tea may be plucked year-round. Continual plucking is strictly dependent on regeneration of new growth; in some years, this may be done as often as every three weeks.

Classic Leaf Styles (Shapes) of Manufactured Green Tea (Dry Leaf)

- Bud-only:
  Sword or sparrow's tongue
- Budset:
  Sword or twisted-needle
- Open or leafy
- Flat or flaky

- Twist
- Spiral or crimped
- Needle or wiry
- Ball or rolled
- Compressed

Green Tea Flavor (Taste) Components

Of all the great classes of tea, green tea requires the most creative and descriptive set of terms for describing its flavor components. Because green teas differ in their processing, they can be as different from one another as they are from black teas.

- Aromatic
- Astringent
- Body—varies
  from light to full
- Bright
- Character
- Clean

- Crisp
- Fresh
- Grassy
- Green
- Herbaceous
- Kelpy
- Lingering finish

- Mineral
- Soft
- Spicy
- Strength
- Sweet
- Vegetal

Gallery of Green Teas

AN JI BAI CHA

REGION: Zhejiang Province, China

MANUFACTURE: Basket-fired

STYLE: Needle leaf

FLAVOR: Sweet, woodsy, and earthy

AROMA: Lingering, fresh, and slightly vegetal

LIQUOR: Clear pale green color

STEEPING: Two or three 2-minute infusions at 170° to 180°F. Drink plain.

An Ji Bai Cha has the quintessential flavor of the high-mountain green teas of eastern China. An Ji Bai Cha is comprised of long, slender, needle-shaped leaves that feature a distinctive lengthwise pleat. Leaf shaped like this often dangles in the water while steeping if there is enough vertical height to allow movement of the leaf into that position. Green tea from the eastern mountains of China has clarity and a fresh taste, and is a rare treat when of premium quality.

GENMAICHA

REGION: Japan, particularly Shizuoka prefecture

MANUFACTURE: Oven-fired (roasted)

STYLE: Needle leaf, with toasted brown rice added

FLAVOR: Toasty and nutty, but clean

AROMA: Spicy, warm, with hints of roasted rice

LIQUOR: Clear green color, tinged with an olive hue

STEEPING: Two or three 2-minute infusions at 170° to 180°F. Drink plain.

Genmaicha, also Genmai Cha, is one of the most established teas of Japan, especially among youthful tea drinkers; its popularity has spread to tea enthusiasts in the West.

Manufactured by blending grains of toasted brown rice (both whole and popped) with either Sencha or Bancha leaf, Genmaicha can be exquisite or just okay. When well made, the deep, vegetal flavor of a high-quality Sencha, combined with the toastiness of perfectly roasted artisanal brown rice, offers a glorious beverage. Genmaicha can be sipped just for pleasure, and it is one of the few teas that marries well with East Asian foods both savory and sweet.

GUNPOWDER (Imperial Pinhead)

REGION: Zhejiang Province, China

MANUFACTURE: Tumble-fired

STYLE: Rolled leaf

FLAVOR: Hearty, but sweet

AROMA: Robust, slightly flinty

LIQUOR: Classic straw color, tinged with an amber hue

STEEPING: Two 3- to 4-minute infusions at 175° to 185°F. Drink plain
  (or use as the base for North African–style minted tea).

Gunpowder tea is one of the best-known and most liked of all the standard green teas. Although it is complicated to manufacture, even the higher grades are inexpensive. Gunpowder tea is one of the most forgiving green teas to prepare. It is easy to measure, will tolerate a range of water temperature, and is fun to watch infuse. Gunpowder tea is the base tea used most commonly for the minted tea of North Africa. Not only does it travel to and store well in a hot and dry climate, but it also infuses slowly, in tandem with the mint.

GYOKURO (Jade Dew)

REGION: Japan, particularly Fukuoka and Kyoto (Uji) prefectures

MANUFACTURE: Steamed and oven-fired (roasted)

STYLE: Twisted needle

FLAVOR: Robust and vegetal

AROMA: Fresh, kelpy, and "green"

LIQUOR: Pale emerald color

STEEPING: Infuse no more than 2 minutes at a maximum 165°F
(a second steeping is possible using even cooler water).
Drink plain.

Gyokuro is the connoisseur's Japanese green tea; its flavor stimulates the palate and engages all the senses. Gyokuro is highly revered in Japan for purity of flavor, depth of the "green" taste, and the robust breadth of flavor that is so unique to Japanese tea. It is one of the few Japanese teas still plucked by hand. Covered with a *tana* (natural reed or plastic netting) for its final period of growth, the chlorophyll content of Gyokuro's fresh leaf increases, providing a softer, sweeter, and more complex flavor than that of the simpler Sencha.

LONGJING (Dragonwell)

REGION: Zhejiang Province, China

MANUFACTURE: Pan-fired

STYLE: Sword budset, or sparrow's tongue bud-only

FLAVOR: Soft, rich, and toasty

AROMA: Full, deep, and chestnutlike

LIQUOR: Straw-colored, tending toward amber with a tea-oil sheen

STEEPING: Two or three 2-minute infusions at 170° to 180°F. Drink plain.

One of China's Ten Famous Teas (those teas previously only enjoyed by the Emperor), Longjing is perhaps China's most beloved green tea. Longjing has a toasty, yeasty flavor with delicate chestnut overtones. Fired in woklike pans over wood charcoal, Longjing tea is created by artisans who are masters of their craft. "Competition-grade" Longjing (which may even be village-specific) is traditionally manufactured into either tiny flattened budsets or bird's beak shapes—seek these out in mid-spring. High-quality, first-grade Longjing is comprised of flattened budsets that have a characteristic straw-yellow tinge. All are distinctive and in China may be purchased in sealed boxes with provenance.

LU AN GUAPIAN (Lu'An Melon Seeds)

REGION: Anhui Province, China

MANUFACTURE: Basket-fired

STYLE: Open leaf

FLAVOR: Earthy, clean, and soft

AROMA: Minerally, yielding to biscuit

LIQUOR: Deep straw color

STEEPING: Two or three 2-minute infusions at 160° to 170°F. Drink plain.

After being rehydrated during steeping, these individual leaves resemble melon seeds of a uniform size and color. The Chinese call melon seeds *guapian* and believe that anything related to the squash family is lucky and fortuitous and promotes fertility. This is a very difficult tea to manufacture. It must be plucked very carefully because it consists of only the single first true leaf below the budset. Specific-leaf field plucking such as this requires significant coordination between the pickers and the tea master on the day of harvest. This leaf is treasured for its concentration of flavor and lack of extraneous moisture.

MATCHA

REGION: Aichi, Kagoshima, Kyoto, and Shizuoka prefectures; Japan

MANUFACTURE: Oven-fired (roasted)

STYLE: Ground to a fine powder

FLAVOR: Vegetal, intense tea flavor, can be sweet

AROMA: Herbaceous, minerally, tastes of the "essence of tea"

LIQUOR: Varying degrees of bright, jade-green color

STEEPING: For *koicha*, use 2 teaspoons of matcha to 2 ounces of water. For *usucha*, use 1 level teaspoon of matcha to 3 ounces of water. Water temperature should be 160° to 180°F. Place the matcha powder in a *chawan* or wide tea bowl and add the water. Use a Japanese bamboo whisk to stir the tea and dissolve it in the water. After the tea is dissolved, carefully increase the intensity of the whisking until the surface of the tea has a nice frothy appearance.

Matcha is one of the more intricately manufactured green teas. Throughout history, tea in powdered form has resurfaced periodically, as the base ingredient for a beverage made from freshly fabricated powdered leaf. It was once compressed into cakes; today, two types of matcha are generally found, either vacuum-packed in a foil pouch or sealed in a small tin: "ceremonial" grade for use in *Chanoyu*, the Japanese Tea Ceremony, and "culinary" grade, for cooking, baking, and everyday drinking. The prices will be wildly different as will the intensity of flavor and the vividness of the color. The variables are the source of the leaf, the expertise and reputation of the tea company, and the consistency of the grind.

Made to exacting standards by several tea companies throughout Japan, ceremonial-grade matcha is exquisite in style and flavor. In order to avoid the occasional harshness and intentional underlying bitterness of most Japanese green teas, the bushes that produce tencha (the leaf used for premium-quality matcha) are more mature, often more than thirty years old. This leaf tends to be mellower, with prominent veining in its relatively large leaves.

Tea plants destined to produce tencha are enclosed in a shade covering for three weeks before harvest. The pluck

is steamed to prevent oxidation, and each leaf is individually stemmed and deveined. The tencha leaf is not rolled, but simply dried and then reserved for grinding into this highest-quality matcha.

As tradition dictates, stone mills are used for grinding matcha. These mills are specially designed to remain cool during the lengthy process of grinding the particles of tencha leaf into a fine powder.

Made to consistent standards by many tea growers, culinary-grade matcha is light in body and mild in flavor. Although from good-quality leaf, the flavor will not be as distinct and the color will not be as intense. Overall, culinary-grade matcha is a wonderful product and a good value, but not as singular as ceremonial-grade matcha. It is used for confections, ice cream, sauces, and baking; it is also used to make a modestly priced cup of sipping tea.

There are two ways that matcha is prepared in *Chanoyu*, and each preparation requires matcha that is specifically made for that use: *koicha* ("thick tea") or *usucha* ("thin tea"). *Koicha* is served in full-length *Chanoyu* gatherings. *Koicha* is an opaque, jade-green, slightly viscous, and deeply flavored drink (see page 51, top). It is traditionally offered in a communal matcha bowl, called a *chawan*. Each guest sips from the *chawan* and then wipes the rim of the bowl where he or she sipped before passing it to the next guest.

Usucha is a light, refreshing, and astringent drink (see page 51, bottom). Although not as popular for everyday tea drinking as Sencha is, matcha prepared as "thin tea" is drunk regularly by many Japanese. In short-form *Chanoyu*, *usucha* is presented in an individual bowl to each guest who must turn the bowl so that the "face" of the bowl can be seen by the other guests before the first sip is taken.

PAN LONG YIN HAO
(Curled Dragon Silver Tips)

REGION: Zhejiang Province, China

MANUFACTURE: Pan-fired

STYLE: Spiral leaf showing significant tip

FLAVOR: Vegetal and assertive

AROMA: Clean, earthy, like an early morning meadow

LIQUOR: Rich straw color

STEEPING: Two or three 2-minute infusions at 170° to 180°F. Drink plain.

Pan Long Yin Hao is a magnificent green tea. Tightly crimped spirals display abundant tip that unfurls to sizable leaf during steeping. Pan Long Yin Hao is one of the smoothest but most-highly flavored green teas that you will encounter. Prepared by either the pan-firing or "column of air" drying method, Pan Long Yin Hao is only produced in limited quantities each year. Be sure to seek out the authentic version from Zhejiang Province.

SENCHA

REGION: Grown in most tea-growing prefectures of Japan; Shizuoka produces 40 percent of the country's total

MANUFACTURE: Steamed and oven-fired (roasted)

STYLE: Flat leaf

FLAVOR: Robust and vegetal

AROMA: Vibrant, grassy, and bright

LIQUOR: Light artichoke color, tinged with an olive hue

STEEPING: Infuse no more than 2 minutes at 160° to 170°F (can be steeped again with cooler water). Drink plain.

Sencha is always a blended tea, a combination of leaf carefully chosen by an expert tea blender. Representative of the blender's art, Sencha manufacture is similar to perfumery—part natural ability and part learned skill. Sencha must be steeped carefully, with water that is not too hot, as it can be a fussy tea. It has the wonderfully vegetal "green" flavor so highly regarded in Japan. Sipped from small cups, Sencha is also a fantastic accompaniment to snacks or savory bites—never sweets! Tasting something savory before drinking Sencha helps highlight the inherent sweetness of the tea.

TAI PING HOU KUI

REGION: Anhui Province, China

MANUFACTURE: Successively pan-fired and basket-fired

STYLE: Flat, needle, very large leaf

FLAVOR: Earthy, rich, and vegetal

AROMA: Toasty, with mosslike wisps

LIQUOR: Deep straw color

STEEPING: Two or three 2-minute infusions at 170° to 180°F. Drink plain.

Tai Ping Hou Kui is one of the Ten Famous Teas of Chinese tea tradition. Grown in a protected area bordering the pristine Tai Ping Lake just north of the Huang Shan, this is one of very few teas that is both pan-fired and basket-fired, blotted in between with the rice paper made locally for calligraphy and scroll painting. The impression of the weave of this paper can be seen on finished Tai Ping Hou Kui leaf. Tai Ping Hou Kui bushes are tended by the local residents whose tea "gardens" are less cultivated and more natural in appearance than the sculpted gardens seen elsewhere. Many of them are "wild growing" with little interference by the workers.

Tips for Purchasing Green Tea

Well-known Chinese green teas such as An Ji Bai Cha, Longjing, and Tai Ping Hou Kui are usually sold under the traditional Chinese name of the tea. Chinese tea enthusiasts inherently know the origin of these teas (province and subregion), and they have an expectation of what the plucking standard will be.

For instance, some famous teas are closely identified by their shape, such as:

- Gunpowder (ball-rolled leaf)
- Longjing (short, flattened budset)
- Pan Long Yin Hao (curled, spiral budset)
- Tai Ping Hou Kui (two very large, flat leaves and a bud)

When purchasing a green tea, seek out as much information as you can about its province and region, the season of the pluck, and the plucking standard. The more information offered means the more definitive the sourcing of the tea will have been.

A famous Chinese tea should have its name meaningfully transliterated into the language of the country in which it is being sold. These teas will be named first by whichever name is believed to be the name by which the tea is best known to that store's clientele. Without this, a tea may still be delicious, but it can be difficult to discover its source or to locate the same tea again. Less-famous teas will be named by one of the several naming conventions noted below.

For illustration, the following are good examples of the information you will encounter. When purchasing a particular Chinese tea in an English-speaking country, it should (or will most likely) be identified according to one of the following:

1. **Descriptive, English name-based identification**
   a. Name of the tea in English, transliterated into "simple" Chinese (i.e., Jing Mt. Silver Tips [Jing Shan Hao Ya])
   b. Name of the tea in English only, origin of name may be solely poetic and not reflective of the Chinese name (i.e., After the Snow Falling)

2. **Authentic, Chinese name-based identification**
    a. Name of the tea only (i.e., Cui Zhu [Bamboo Tips])
    b. Name above, plus the name of the province (i.e., Cui Zhu [Bamboo Tips], Sichuan Province)
    c. Name above, plus the name of the specific village or mountain of origin within the province (i.e., Cui Zhu [Bamboo Tips], Emei Shan, Sichuan Province)

3. **Authentic, Chinese name-only identification**
    a. When a tea is well-known by its Chinese name, that name may be used alone (i.e., Longjing)

GRADES OF GREEN TEA

The language used to designate grades of green tea can differ widely, and even lack meaning, because no national or universal standard exists for grading green tea. This lack of standardization can present confusion when several vendors use different terms for what may be the same grade of tea. For example, some vendors use the term *imperial* to designate the top grade of a particular tea; other vendors label that same grade of tea as *premium*. Insufficient terminology can make it difficult to know whether you are being offered the same tea, different grades of the same tea, or two entirely different teas from harvests of different weeks, months, or places when comparison shopping from several tea vendors. None of this may matter if the tea is sound and offered at a fair price, but tea buyers should be aware that complexity is the norm.

Without clear and consistent grades, it can be difficult for a tea enthusiast to know whether a certain tea is more expensive than another because it is overpriced or because it is a higher grade. There will be no resolution of this because the tea industry cannot possibly codify the thousands of green teas available, so it is necessary to cultivate a relationship with a tea vendor whom you trust. As you become familiar with their teas, you will in essence become familiar with their palate and their criteria for selection. This will prove to be more valuable to your enjoyment of tea than any complex, universal system of standards could ever be.

To knowledgeably select a green tea, a tea enthusiast should be familiar with several grading fundamentals. As with several other foods, most notably wine, cheese, coffee, and olive oil, the complexity of identifying and codifying the differences between various tea offerings can seem daunting. However, with a little basic knowledge it becomes fairly easy to distinguish among the teas available and find a selection that meets a particular need. Premium green teas tend to follow a specific plucking standard, are plucked early in the spring, and have certain country-specific particulars.

BUYING GREEN TEA FROM CHINA

Chinese green teas are offered by place of origin, pluck, manufactured shape, and season of harvest. Historically, specific locations offer prime conditions for particular subvarieties of tea bushes and are famous for that tea. Some growing areas feature a variety of bushes and styles of above-average quality. In every instance, premium Chinese green tea starts with the leaf on the bush, and then the other variables of handling and manufacture come into play. Every China tea bush subvariety and cultivar will tend to a certain shape and style of finished tea; encouraging that development is the challenge presented to the tea maker.

These are the key elements that should be identified regarding a Chinese spring-pluck green tea.

1. **Time of the pluck (for seasonal spring tea)**
   - Pre-Qing Ming or Ming Qian tea (before April 5)
        Ex: 2009 pre-Qing Ming Longjing Dafo Village
   - Before the Rains or Yu Qian tea (before April 20)
   - Spring tea or Gu Yu tea (before May 6)
   - Late Spring tea or Li Xia tea (before May 21)

2. **Plucking standard (the configuration of buds and leaves of the pluck)**
   - *Ya* (bud only, or "tips")
        Ex: Huang Shan Cui Ya

- *Mao jian* (bud and one leaf)
     Ex: Xin Yang Mao Jian
- *Mao feng* (bud and two leaves)
     Ex: Huang Shan Mao Feng

Not All Longjing Is Created Equally

The following listing shows the very precise grading system for authentic West Lake (Xi Hu) Longjing tea as devised by the City of Hangzhou in 2005. Accordingly, eight grades of Longjing from three designated places—Shi Feng, Meijiawu Village, and West Lake Village—are classified, and as you can see from the first three grades, the devil is in the details. When purchasing a premium tea that has such a pedigree (and subsequent wildly fluctuating prices), shop wisely by tasting or purchasing a small quantity first, and always procure the finest example that you can afford.

1. AAA Jing Pin: 100 percent bud and one leaf
2. AA Te Ji: 70 percent bud and one leaf, 30 percent one bud and two leaves
3. Grade #1: 70 percent one bud and two leaves; 30 percent bud and one leaf
4. Grade #2
5. Grade #3
6. Grade #4
7. Grade #5
8. Grade #6

BUYING GREEN TEA FROM JAPAN

Because most Japanese green tea is blended (not so the tea from small independent tea farmers), it is purchased by tea enthusiasts for its taste and price—not primarily by origin, as with Chinese green teas. As in the West, tea companies in Japan compete for the loyalty of Japanese green tea drinkers via their "house" teas. These teas have been created by master blenders who have established and are then charged with maintaining a trademark flavor.

In Japan, tea is sold under the following specifics:

1. The tea producer
   Ex: Ippodo
2. The type of tea
   Ex: Sencha, Gyokuro, Shincha
3. Plus a colorful identity name
   Ex: Sencha "Eijyu" or Sencha "Kazemiyabi"
4. Plus the prefecture or region
   Ex: Sayama Sencha "Eijyu," Saitama prefecture
   or Honyama Sencha "Kazemiyabi," Shizuoka
   prefecture
5. By the season of the pluck
   Ex: Shincha, Ichibancha, Nibancha, Sanbancha,
   or Yobancha
6. And by grade
   Ex: ultra premium, extra premium, premium,
   high quality

BUYING GREEN TEA FROM KOREA

Everyday green tea is commonly referred to as *nok-cha* in Korea. Early spring teas plucked from slender leaves such as those from Ujeon, Sejak, and Jungjak are classified as *jakseol*, or "sparrow's tongue," a term that alludes to the tiny size of the leaves.

Korean green tea is sold under the name of the producer and usually by season of the year in which it was plucked. Poetic names may also be given, such as Sweetness of the Morning, Spring Dew, and so on. For example:

1. The tea producer
   Ex: Hankook
2. The season of the pluck
   Ex: Ujeon (earliest pluck, end of April) or
   Sejak (second pluck, beginning of May)
3. Plus a colorful identity name
   Ex: Ujeon "Gamro" or Sejak "Teuk Seon"
4. Plus the region
   Ex: Hwagea Valley or Boseong County

The Perfect Cup: Specifics for Steeping Green Tea

Green teas are the herald of spring, a sign that the anticipated rejuvenation of the earth from the icy grip of winter is beginning. Tea shops in Asia clear off the shelves for the arrival of the first teas of the new season: pre-Qing Ming teas in China, Shincha in Japan, and Ujeon in Korea. These teas fill the mouth with fresh, delicious flavors that are sweet and refreshing, like a much-needed breath of fresh air.

Following these teas, the mid-spring teas arrive in the marketplace. Being more delicate than most other classes of tea, green teas require steeping water that has cooled from the boil. Water that is too hot will force the leaf to become bitter, rather than encourage it to yield the sweetness inherent in the leaf.

MEASUREMENTS	
Tea Type	**Amount (per 6 ounces of water)**
Green teas from China	1 to 2 tablespoons for leafy tea; 1 to 2 teaspoons for bud tea
Green teas from Japan	1 to 2 teaspoons
Green teas from Korea	1 to 2 tablespoons

WATER TEMPERATURE	
Tea Type	**Temperature**
Spring green teas from China	160° to 170°F
Green teas from Japan	160° to 170°F
Green teas from China	170° to 180°F
Green teas from Korea	170° to 180°F

STEEPING TIME
90 seconds to 2 minutes

NUMBER OF STEEPINGS
One to three

The preceding measurements will work whether you are using a *gaiwan*, an individual teacup or mug, or a teapot, and can be scaled up directly. When you become familiar with a tea, adjust the specifics to your taste.

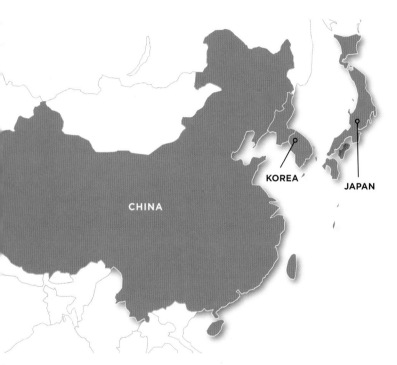

Major Tea-Producing Countries and Regions: Green Tea

The Role of Green Tea

Green tea reminds us that food is a reflection of the essential alliance between earth and man. Artisan, handmade green tea is a labor of love on the part of the tea maker, which results in a blissful tea-drinking experience.

The finest green teas are:

- Produced from the hand-plucked buds and tiny leaves of tea bushes awakening in the earliest days of spring
- Selected from vigorous, healthy tea plants
- Hand-plucked at the correct month, week, or day necessary for the style of tea

- Carefully sorted to remove imperfect or torn leaf, bits of stem, and miscellaneous waste
- Precisely shaped by hand or shaping machines
- Finish-fired over a controlled heat source by experienced workers.

GREEN TEA IN CHINA

China has a very long history and tradition of green tea manufacture—in fact, it was the Chinese who discovered the measures necessary to turn fresh leaf into green tea. China dominates worldwide production of green tea, not only in the sheer volume of leaf produced each year, but also in the seemingly endless number of local green tea varieties that are contributed to the collective whole by the small tea making villages in China's green tea–producing provinces.

China's best teas are made by tea workers using skilled hands, as well as the experience that their eyes, ears, and noses bring to the task of tea making. Making tea by hand requires dedication, skill, and patience. While machinery assists some tea workers with their task, machines cannot determine how to make the precise, spontaneous adjustments that many teas require.

In 2007, China produced 1,165 metric tons of tea, surpassing the production of India for the first time in many years. Of this, approximately 70 percent of China's yearly output of tea was green tea. And of this, only 10 to 12 percent was premium, artisan, spring-plucked green tea. It is believed that there are almost ten thousand distinctions of green tea produced in China's eastern provinces of Anhui, Henan, Hunan, Jiangsu, Jiangxi, and Zhejiang and the western provinces of Sichuan, Guizhou, and Yunnan.

China's most delicious green teas are delicate, fresh, and clean. Some possess vegetal flavors in the cup, like fresh bamboo or artichoke; others are earthy, grassy, and minerally in style, reflecting the cool climate and austere soil (*terroir*) found high in the tea mountains.

How Gunpowder Tea Got Its Name

Gunpowder tea is so named because the finished tea resembles the steel-gray-green color and pellet shape of the propellant gunpowder. Additionally, the ball-shaped finished tea pellets gently "pop open" when exposed to the steeping water, and the stimulant nature of tea could be construed as a pun on the term *propellant*. Both are of Chinese invention, so it was most likely an observant foreigner who first coined the term for use describing the tea, or perhaps there was once a very improperly labeled container that must have been a disappointment for the recipient who expected an armament supply and received tea by mistake! Picture an English ship's captain plying the waters of the South China Sea in the 1800s, and imagine his disdain trying to fire his cannons at marauding pirates with only slow-burning Gunpowder tea!

GREEN TEA IN JAPAN

Most green tea consumed in Japan is produced on this small but intensively farmed country of islands. Japanese tea enthusiasts are deeply connected to the flavor of Japanese green tea and are rarely attracted to the green tea offerings of other countries.

The flavor of Japanese tea is vivid, striking, and vegetal, which makes it unique among green teas and deliciously refreshing any time of day. In the cup, the best Japanese teas feature both astringency and sweetness in equal measure, a highly desirable and controllable attribute of green tea that has been finely honed by Japanese tea artisans.

In contrast to China, Japan historically produces only one major class of tea—green tea. Japan is famous for dark, forest green, thin, needle-shaped green teas that are uniquely Japanese in style and flavor. Underscoring this selective focus is the additional fact that Japanese tea makers produce only a scant handful of green tea varieties, a distinction that sharply contrasts the Japanese green tea industry with that of neighboring China.

In Japan, the tea need not have a fanciful appearance, hence there is not the multitude of shapes (twists, curls, balls, and so on) that Chinese green tea exhibits. With the exception of well-loved and famous teas that are tied to a certain place, such as Gyokuro from Uji in Kyoto prefecture, emphasis is not on specific tea gardens or famous mountains, but on distinctions that differentiate the teas from larger geographic areas, such as Shizuoka, Kyushu, and central Honshu.

Japanese tea enthusiasts are intensely focused on fresh, vibrant flavor and the preservation of flavor throughout the season. In Japan, tea should exhibit three necessary characteristics: good aroma, good taste, and good appearance.

GREEN TEA IN KOREA

The exact dating of the introduction of green tea to Korea is difficult to determine, but awareness of tea is believed to have reached the Gaya Kingdom (today, part of South Korea) around 48 AD. As tea developed in China and Japan, tea and tea drinking were most likely emphasized in Korea by monks returning from study at China's great Buddhist schools and temples. It is reported that King Heungdeok (r. 826–836) planted tea seeds on Jiri Mountain and that King TaeJo, the first ruler of the Koryo dynasty (918–1392) gave tea as gifts to priests, monks, and military leaders.

Korea's tea industry is small. For most of the mid- to late twentieth century, the beverages of choice in Korea were coffee or roasted grain beverages made from corn, barley, and rice. Today, interest in *Camellia sinensis* and in Korea's unique history with tea is beginning to rekindle.

Plucking Style for Green Tea

In China, Japan, and Korea, leaf for green tea is plucked beginning in the spring when the tea bushes are awakening from their winter dormancy, fresh with vital plant nutrients and energy (*qi*).

PLUCKING STYLE IN CHINA

In China, leaf for green tea is traditionally hand-plucked. In all of the green tea–producing provinces of China, leaf for green tea is plucked by hand by legions of workers who comb through the tea fields daily or twice daily gathering fresh leaf. The Chinese do a "fine plucking," which means that the workers pluck only the specific leaf or leaf set that the tea-factory manager wants for the type of tea that will be made from that day's fresh leaf.

Some teas, such as the famous Chinese green teas, are only picked once a year during the spring. And spring itself is broken up into early, mid-, and late spring. For these teas, the smallest buds and leaves are gathered and timing is of the essence. The younger and smaller the leaf, the finer, more delicious, and more costly the tea will be.

Chinese wisdom in the tea garden dictates, "Tea that is picked early is a treasure; picked late, it's trash." Because green, yellow, and white teas are processed so minimally, the size of the leaf before manufacture has a critical impact on the flavor of the finished tea.

PLUCKING STYLE IN JAPAN

A tiny amount of artisan tea is hand-plucked, but most leaf is machine-sheared. For Japan to produce the quantity of tea that it needs, leaf plucking must be efficient and quick. Japanese tea production is a modern industry, and machine-shearing is an efficient way to obtain the highest yield.

A Japanese leaf shearer may be able to harvest two hundred to three hundred pounds of tea per day, while a tea plucker in a Chinese tea garden may only net twenty to thirty pounds of leaves per day plucking by hand. While shearing does not allow for precise leaf plucking, it does result in all-over "even" leaf growth and ensures that the maximum usable leaf will be trimmed from the bushes each time.

Nevertheless, some Japanese teas (Gyokuro, Kabuse, and the leaf grown for tencha) are made from leaf that is both hand-plucked and shade-grown. Canopies called *tanas* are set up over and around the tea bushes (after the bushes have been growing in full sun) for several weeks, right up to the time of harvest. This technique produces Japan's famous shade-grown tea, and it alters the chemistry of the plant, forcing it to produce an extra abundance of chlorophyll. Unique even among Japanese green teas, leaf grown by this method is costly and has a high degree of complexity and sweetness in its flavor.

PLUCKING STYLE IN KOREA

While leaf is primarily machine-sheared in the large commercial tea gardens, a small quantity of hand-plucked wild tea is still gathered. In general, the Korean tea industry is modern, and most gardens were developed in the twentieth century (except for the temple gardens in Hadong County).

Many lush, cultivated tea gardens were developed by the Japanese during their occupation of Korea before their departure at the end of World War II. Located in the South Korean counties of Haenam, Yeongam, and Jangseong of southern Jelloanam Province, these tea gardens provide mainly machine-plucked tea, but occasionally some handmade tea can be found. Jeju Island contributes a quantity of mass-produced, lesser-quality green tea.

In South Gyeongsang Province, Hadong County, Hwagae Valley (especially Jiri Mountain) has famous Buddhist temples and tea fields that blanket this narrow valley and its mountainsides. Here, leaf is hand-plucked from "wild" tea bushes, that is, bushes that are descendents of the original tea bushes planted from seed centuries ago by monks in the hills near the Ssanggyesa Temple. These are considered indigenous tea bushes, in contrast to modern clonal varieties of tea bushes that were planted as cuttings in other parts of South Korea.

Hadong tea is grown without pesticides, but is made in small amounts and will prove difficult to find outside Korea. Because of the relatively small amount of handmade tea in

Korea, the best teas are very costly. However, Korea's cultivated tea is well worth seeking out. It is uniquely different from Chinese and Japanese green teas, with a flavor all its own. Look for tea that has been made in the earliest days of spring, when the leaf is most tender and sweet.

The Harvest Year: Seasonal Plucks for Green Tea

Each tea is plucked according to a plucking standard for that tea. The standard will change as the harvest season progresses, and each successive tea is made from larger and slightly older leaf. Even though a plucking standard is applied to successive plucks throughout the year, the small leaves of the spring plucks ensure the sweetest tea.

HARVEST YEAR IN CHINA

Specific to China bush *Camellia sinensis* var. *sinensis* (which goes dormant over the winter months), new leaf growth represents the fresh taste of spring: the essence of flavor that develops within the plant during the winter months.

Over the course of spring, four seasonal plucks will occur before the rainy season arrives and summer plucking commences. Not all green tea is plucked four times during the spring season: some teas are only plucked twice during the earliest weeks of spring.

The summer and fall harvests are important crops; these comprise the bulk of China's ordinary, standard green tea. There is almost always a single pluck in the fall, when conditions replicate the weather, daylight, and general atmosphere of spring. Often high in quality, the yield is small due to the pressure of the intensive summer harvest.

Most agricultural practices in Asia are measured against a calendar that is based on movements or divisions of the sun in relation to the position of the earth. In the solar calendar, twenty-four seasonal divisions (or mini-seasons) mark the expected dates of natural occurrences in segments of fifteen days spaced through-out the twelve months of the year.

These markers also act as pointers for guiding farmers when to plant and harvest crops. For green tea, timing is everything. The season moves quickly once the plants begin to send out new shoots. The shoots grow larger each day, opening into a set of two leaves that will continue to grow larger as new shoots develop. In some cases, tea that is made one week can no longer be made ten days later. This underscores why it is that the younger the green tea leaf, the better the quality and the more costly the tea will be in the marketplace.

Tea-important highlights of the Chinese calendar are:

- **Chufen,** the fourth solar division (coinciding with the vernal equinox around March 21), marks bud break and the time to pluck the tender new tea buds. These teas are known as pre-Qing Ming, or *Ming Qian* in Chinese.
- **Qing Ming,** the fifth solar division (approximately April 5 to April 20), brings a major flush of sweet green teas to market. Elongating leaves augment the buds, creating the budset plucks: *mao jian* and *mao feng*. Teas picked during this divi-sion are called Before the Rain, or *Yu Qian*, teas.
- **Gu Yu,** the sixth solar division (approximately April 20 to May 6), marks the time when the tea leaves are growing quite vig-orously, and the pluck changes from budset to leaf. Tea from this division is known simply as Spring, or *Gu Yu*, tea.
- **Lixia,** the seventh solar division (May 6 to May 21), marks the beginning of the rainy season. Tea from this division is known as Late Spring, or *Lixia*, tea. After this date the tea is classified as summer tea and will consist of many different pluck styles.

HARVEST YEAR IN JAPAN

The arrival of Shincha in tea shops each spring heralds the new Japanese tea season. The rush to market to acquire this precious new tea is impressive. Shincha exemplifies the notion that each tea exists for only a fleeting moment in time and that one tea must yield to another successive tea until the same season returns the following year. Happily for Japanese tea enthusiasts, each successive week of the tea season brings new tea tastes to market. The Japanese tea season follows closely those of China and Korea:

- **Shincha:** new tea, limited early plucking from *Seimei* (early April)
- **Ichibancha:** first plucking from *Rikka* (mid-May)
- **Nibancha:** second plucking from *Geshi* (end of June)
- **Sanbancha:** third plucking from *Risshū* (mid-August)
- **Yobancha:** fourth plucking from *Shūbun* (late September)

HARVEST YEAR IN KOREA

Korea also follows an agricultural solar calendar that references the position of the sun, and most tea is sold by a name that designates the season during which it was plucked. As with other East Asian green teas, the earlier in the season the leaf is plucked, the more succulent and delicious the tea will be. Accordingly, the Korean tea season is as follows:

- **Ujeon** (a bud and single leaf) is the first pluck of the season, which usually occurs just before *Koku* (first grain rain and sixth seasonal division: around April 20).
- **Sejak** (a bud and two leaves) is plucked during *Ipha* (start of summer: around May 6).
- **Jungjak** (third plucking, no bud) occurs during *Soman* (full grains season: around May 21).
- **Deajak,** Korea's ordinary green tea, is plucked during the summer months.

Leaf Manufacture: Production Methods for Green Tea

Green tea manufacture is broadly divided into two categories: **de-enzymed green tea** (Chinese style, Korean style) and **steamed green tea** (Japanese style, Korean style).

All fresh leaf being manufactured into finished green tea must be taken to a tea "factory," which can range from a small, simple stone or concrete structure in a rural tea village to an immense modern factory, but both are centrally located for servicing its tea-growing region. During transport and after arrival at the factory, the leaf will shed a small amount of surface moisture. This initial moisture loss allows the leaf to become pliable, which prevents damage to the leaf during the various steps of manufacture.

Following this softening, the leaf is manufactured and dried as quickly as possible to achieve maximum flavor. The best green tea leaf is kept intact to keep the internal cell juices locked inside the leaf until they are released into the cup on contact with hot water during steeping. Green tea manufacture can be accomplished with several shaping and drying processes. The most widely used are:

- Basket-firing
- Oven-baking or roasting
- Pan-firing
- Sun-drying
- Tumble-drying

Additionally, depending on the manufacturing style being used, hand- or machine-rolling may be necessary to shape the leaf into its distinctive appearance. Lastly, finish-firing (or final-drying), which brings the moisture content of the leaf down to a shelf-stable level, is completed either as a part of the manufacture (as in basket- or pan-firing) or as a separate step, in which case "finishing" is usually accomplished by oven-baking or tumble-drying.

GREEN TEA PRODUCTION METHODS IN CHINA

Chinese green teas are made by one of two methods: **artisan tea** (handwork combined with the use of some machinery) and **commercial tea** (primarily machine-made).

Chinese green tea artisans possess hand skills that no others have. Each tea-producing region is celebrated for particular teas that feature fancifully shaped and visually eye-catching leaves. The dry leaf may be a tiny bud pluck (which is also known as a "bird's beak" or "sparrow's tongue" shape) showing the soft olive-green color of early spring. Other teas may be shaped into a classic "sword" or an elongated needle-shaped leaf; the latter tends to float upright while steeping. Basket-fired teas are curled and twisted, reflecting both the judicious manipulation by experienced hands during the rolling process and the inherent resiliency of the leaf's structure. Pan-fired leaf has the reserved look of a starched collar, revealing a flattened budset that thirsts for water to restore its original three-dimensional silhouette.

When the fresh leaf reaches the tea factory, workers quickly shape and dry the leaf. The leaf is put into a cylindrical machine (de-enzymer) that lightly heats the leaf (or it is put into a tea-firing pan) to drive off some initial moisture. This heat is only enough to dry the surface of the leaf so that it becomes pliable, and it kills any bacteria on the leaf that might encourage the development of mold. Most important, this process destroys oxidative enzymes in the leaf that would allow oxidation to begin.

Next, the fresh leaf—now called "primary tea"—is put into a tea-firing pan or tea-firing basket. The tea firers expose the leaf to heat for a short period, remove it from the heat, and place it on large, flat bamboo trays. Using their hands and nimble fingers, they gently twist, roll, and press the leaf into the appropriate shape. These two steps of heating and shaping are repeated until the leaf retains the necessary shape and is sufficiently dried. In the manufacture of Chinese green tea the handwork and attention to detail is paramount to the success of the batch and the flavor of the tea.

GREEN TEA PRODUCTION METHODS IN JAPAN

Japanese tea production is very modern and utilizes machinery in every step of production. Some factories use computerized systems to keep the process running smoothly; it is only a small percentage of independent tea farmers who still make tea using traditional hand skills, and the cost of these teas is very high.

The fundamental reason Japanese green tea differs from Chinese or Korean green tea is that all fresh leaf entering a Japanese tea factory undergoes a brief steaming. Steaming is how the Japanese de-enzyme their green tea leaf. This step affects both the distinctive flavor and the signature color of Japanese green tea, rendering the color of the leaf rich dark green and the color of the liquor an intense, vivid yellow-green. Japanese green teas have been described as vegetal, kelpy, and chewy—desirable qualities that result from the steaming process.

Another unique aspect of Japanese green tea is that several teas prominently feature the addition of other raw materials added to the leaf. For example, Kukicha Yama is a blend of Sencha leaf and fine, thin-cut stems from the tea bush, and Genmaicha, which is a tasty mix of either Sencha leaf (from spring or summer plucking) or green Bancha leaf (fall plucking) and kernels of roasted and popped rice.

Japan is the primary country that continues the historic tradition of producing finely milled, emerald-green matcha powdered tea. (Matcha is made in China and Korea as well, but neither of these two countries can match the sublime sophistication of flavor and aroma that Japanese matcha producers have attained.) Matcha is milled from tencha, leaf that is specifically manufactured for matcha production.

GREEN TEA PRODUCTION METHODS
IN KOREA

Tea enthusiasts will be richly rewarded if they find a source for artisan, handmade Korean green tea. Traditional, artisan tea production follows one of two main methods: *Puch'o-cha* or *Chung-ch'a*. Both of these methods use de-enzyming, leaf rolling and shaping, drying, and parching steps, but the production methods used for each are completely different and uniquely Korean.

Puch'o-cha is parched or lightly roasted tea that is made in a fashion similar to China's pan-fired teas. First, the fresh leaf is de-enzymed in a tea-firing pan to drive excess moisture from the leaf, then the leaf is removed from the pan and vigorously rolled and shaped on a flat bamboo or straw mat. Clumps of leaves are separated by hand, and the leaf is allowed to air-dry for a short period of time.

After the leaf has rested and cooled a bit, it is returned to the tea-firing pan and heated again. This procedure will be repeated as many times as the tea master determines necessary.

Lastly, the leaf will sit at room temperature for as long as overnight before receiving a final parching in a tea-firing pan (at a lower temperature). This final step gives the tea taste, enhances fragrance, and releases the character of the tea.

The second method, *Chung-ch'a*, is the time-honored, traditional way to make tea in Korea. This unique process incorporates both Japanese and Chinese tea-making techniques. The fresh leaf is quickly submerged in near-boiling water to de-enzyme, then it is removed and drained, after which it is painstakingly hand-rolled and shaped in a tea-firing pan for hours.

YELLOW TEA

Yellow teas are unique to the high mountain regions of the Chinese provinces of Anhui, Hunan, and Sichuan. In China, yellow tea is known as *huang ya*, and this unique and specialized leaf manufacture has been rewarded with its own classification.

Unfortunately, yellow teas are not very well known in the West, so some yellow teas are miscategorized as green tea. This is understandable, as most yellow teas are bud and leaf teas that very closely resemble some green teas in appearance.

Classic Leaf Styles (Shapes) of Manufactured Yellow Tea (Dry Leaf)

- Bud-only: Sword or sparrow's tongue
- Budset: Sword or twisted-needle

Yellow Tea Flavor (Taste) Components

Yellow tea is processed almost the same as is green tea, but an extra processing step mellows it and softens its assertiveness.

- Aromatic
- Body—medium
- Bright
- Clean
- Fresh
- Smooth
- Soft

Gallery of Yellow Teas

HUO SHAN HUANG YA
(Yellow Sprouting)

REGION: Anhui Province, China

MANUFACTURE: Basket-fired plus *men huan* ("sealing yellow")

STYLE: Twisted-needle budset

FLAVOR: Pure, mildly "waxy"

AROMA: Softly herbaceous, reminiscent of sweetgrass

LIQUOR: Clear straw color

STEEPING: Two or three 2-minute infusions at 170° to 175°F. Drink plain.

Huo Shan Huang Ya still uses a *mao jian* pluck (bud and one leaf) for its manufacture. Grown on the Huo Shan in the far west of Anhui Province in eastern China, this tea typifies yellow tea as it has been made there for centuries. Leaf from the eastern mountains of China has a clarity and fresh taste that is distinctive. In total, the flavor of Huo Shan Huang Ya is a connoisseur's recipe for the fresh taste of a spring tea tempered by the unmistakable smoothness (known as "waxiness") that is so desirable in a matured, "rested" tea.

MENGDING SHAN HUANG YA
(Mengding Mountain Snow Buds)

REGION: Sichuan Province, China

MANUFACTURE: Pan-fired plus *men huan* ("sealing yellow")

STYLE: Sword-style bud-only tea (often called sparrow's tongue)

FLAVOR: Toasty and brisk, but smooth

AROMA: Clean and invigorating, reminiscent of freshly mown hay

LIQUOR: Clear pale straw color, tinged with pale green

STEEPING: Two or three 2-minute infusions at 170° to 180°F. Drink plain.

Mengding Mountain on the Tibetan Plateau in northwestern
Sichuan Province is likely the birthplace of cultivated tea. The
garden that grows Mengding Shan Huang Ya is located just
northwest of Mount Emei, one of the four sacred mountains
in Chinese Buddhism. The leaf is gathered in the garden as a
bud-only pluck. This elegant tea is slightly toasty and needs
several steepings to really show off its delicious, deep-rooted
flavor profile. The days that we visited Mengding Shan in
spring 2004 it snowed heavily, validating the name "Snow
Buds."

Tips for Purchasing Yellow Tea

Yellow teas should reflect their careful handling and esteemed status. The tea should be clean and handsome (with no broken bits or pieces), uniform in size, and possess good, rich color. Yellow teas are not yellow in color, although they can have a slightly yellowish cast. The color should be vibrant and indicative of being this year's tea.

Some yellow teas might age well, but it is best to experiment on your own with fresh tea that you purchase and age. Decline to purchase yellow tea with a faded, pale color.

The aroma must be fresh and inviting—leaf yellow teas have a tendency to be more aromatic than bud yellow teas, which sometimes have all of their aromatics and flavor turned inward only to be released on steeping. Either way, the aroma should always suggest fresh and new, not old and tired.

The Perfect Cup: Specifics for Steeping Yellow Tea

Yellow teas can steep to a greenish cup or one that is enticingly golden. As with white and green teas, the water temperature should have dropped many degrees off the boil so that scorching does not induce unwanted astringency and ruin the lovely nature of the tea.

Bud yellow teas such as Mengding Shan Huang Ya are dense and compact, while leafy yellow teas such as Huo Shan Huang Ya are light and more voluminous. The volume of each measure needs to be appropriate to the tea being steeped: less for dense bud-only teas (maybe as little as one rounded teaspoon) and more for leafy teas (two tablespoons or more) per six ounces of water.

Yellow teas can be steeped successfully two or three times; much depends on the tea. The *men huan* ("sealing yellow") process locks the flavor inside the leaf; sometimes, especially with tightly formed buds, the flavor needs to be coaxed out over several steepings.

The following measurements will work whether you are using a *gaiwan*, an individual teacup or mug, or a teapot, and can be scaled up directly. When you become familiar with a tea, adjust to your taste.

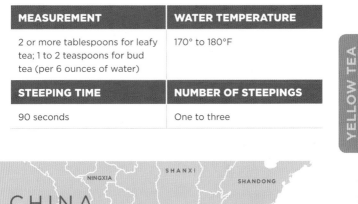

MEASUREMENT	WATER TEMPERATURE
2 or more tablespoons for leafy tea; 1 to 2 teaspoons for bud tea (per 6 ounces of water)	170° to 180°F
STEEPING TIME	**NUMBER OF STEEPINGS**
90 seconds	One to three

Major Tea-Producing Countries and Regions: Yellow Tea

The Role of Yellow Tea

China is the only country that produces yellow tea (Korea produces a tea that is called "yellow tea," but it is a completely different tea and in no way an attempt to duplicate Chinese yellow tea), and the number of yellow teas produced today is fewer than in the past. It is feared that the knowledge needed to process yellow tea is being lost. Many of the tea masters who historically made yellow tea are now retiring or deceased, and in China's rush to produce more green tea to meet Western demand these splendid teas may disappear.

Plucking Style for Yellow Tea

The pluck is critical for yellow tea because it can only be manufactured during the early spring harvest. One technique is to pluck newly formed spring buds before they begin to unfurl into leaves. These buds may be covered with downy fuzz (as are some early spring green teas) or may be smooth and shiny.

In some places, it is traditional to use a very fine *mao feng* pluck of a bud and two tiny leaves (Huang Shan Huang Ya) or a *mao jian* pluck—a budset and one leaf (Huo Shan Huang Ya). Either way, the additional step of *men huan* ("sealing yellow") requires the freshest leaf and a more lengthy processing time.

The Harvest Year: Seasonal Plucks for Yellow Tea

Spring buds are used because they are the juiciest and most tender part of the tea bush. They are filled with the flush of energy and goodness as the tea bushes awaken from winter dormancy. Spring bud teas are believed to contain the highest available amount of antioxidant plant nutrient and are therefore considered to be the most healthful to consume.

It is much more labor-intensive for a tea picker to spend a day plucking buds in the tea garden than it is to fill a basket with plucked leaf—the ratio of buds to leaf is very small. For example, a day's plucking might yield a tea picker eight ounces of buds for yellow tea compared to twenty or more pounds of leaf destined to become green tea.

Leaf Manufacture: Production Methods for Yellow Tea

Once reported to be a favorite of Song Dynasty emperors (960–1279), yellow tea requires the attention of a dedicated tea worker who has a particular "feel" for the way the tea manufacture is progressing.

Yellow teas are made utilizing the following techniques:

- Plucking
- Basket-firing or pan-firing
- Smothering
- Finish-firing

The smothering step, known as *men huan*, or "sealing yellow," is how yellow tea leaf develops its special flavor characteristics. During this step, the leaf is lightly steamed, then removed from the heat source. The leaf is covered with a cloth, which encourages the leaf to reabsorb its own aromatics but also to "breathe" while undergoing the process.

"Sealing yellow" introduces a sweetness and fragrance to the leaf over the course of several hours or several days. The steaming step allows the genius of the tea maker to come into play. For example, details such as how long to steam the tea leaves, how many times to steam or for how many days, how much rest to give the leaf in between each steaming, and how to wrap or cover the steamed leaves while they rest will all affect the final flavor of the tea. The tea master decides the answers to these questions, and it is only after he appraises the fresh leaf and judges its quality and essence that he can determine how he will best execute the *men huan*.

Astringency is reduced, aromatics are enhanced, and the leaf acquires a mature quality from the resting periods. As with most fine artisan-made tea, yellow tea cannot be made by watching the clock or setting a timer—the tea master must decide (by smell, look, and feel) when the process has worked its magic on the leaf. It is this type of tending by a tea master that makes traditional tea making such a craft, and that consistently puts China at the pinnacle of excellence for the production of so many handmade teas.

YELLOW TEA

WHITE TEA

China's Fujian Province is the home of authentic white tea. This mountainous province produces an astonishing treasure chest of incomparable teas; in fact, Fujian is one of only a few provinces in China that produces four of the six classes of tea (plus wood-smoked and flower-scented teas).

White tea is the feather in the jeweled tea cap of Fujian. This is in addition to its production of the powerful and lush Wu Yi Shan and Anxi oolongs, ethereal fresh flower–scented jasmine tea, the elegant Bai Lin Congou and Panyang Congou family of black teas, Tianshan green tea, and the historically important smoky Lapsang Souchong black tea.

Once white tea did come into production in the late 1700s (mid–Qing dynasty, 1644–1911), it was leaf rather than powdered tea that was used to create white tea. Loose-leaf tea was becoming the style of the day, ushering in a new era in which tea was steeped freely in a small teapot. Bud white teas, such as Bai Hao Yin Zhen, however, did not appear until the late 1800s.

Several subvarieties of tea bushes indigenous to the northeast corner of Fujian Province (close to the Zhejiang

border) were deemed to be most proficient at producing juicy, fat buds with an attractive appearance and excellent flavor. The best of these, the Da Bai varieties, were cultivated expressly for the production of shapely white tea buds, which became known as Bai Hao Yin Zhen, or Silver Needles, the most famous white tea in China.

After China's imperial days came to a close in 1911, production of China's famous teas continued. During the 1920s Fujian tea makers began to produce a new style of white tea— Bai Mudan (White Peony)—for export to England. This new tea incorporated leaf from the same bushes into the tea buds and resulted in a white tea that steeped to a stronger flavor.

A further modification to white tea came during the 1960s when additional styles of leafy white teas were created. These modern-style white teas, as they have come to be called, were a variation of Bai Mudan that allowed tea makers to incorporate leaf and buds (in varying proportions) from white tea bushes that were plucked later in the spring.

WHITE TEA

Classic Leaf Styles (Shapes) of Manufactured White Tea (Dry Leaf)

Traditional:
- Bud-only: Sword or sparrow's tongue
- Budset: Sword or twisted-needle

Modern:
- Bud-only: Sword or sparrow's tongue
- Open or leafy

White Tea Flavor (Taste) Components

In general, white tea is smooth and mellow due to its light oxidation.

- Body—full
- Clean
- Short-finished
- Smooth
- Soft
- Sweet

Gallery of White Teas

BAI HAO YIN ZHEN (Silver Needles)

REGION: Fujian Province, China

MANUFACTURE: Air-dried white tea (about 5 percent oxidation), sometimes with a finish-fire bake-drying

STYLE: Full buds with downy hairs; may be short and plump or long and slender

FLAVOR: Smooth, sweet, and soft

AROMA: Clean, floral, and sweet

LIQUOR: Pale tending to a silver color

STEEPING: Numerous 2- to 3-minute infusions at 160° to 170°F. Drink plain.

Bai Hao Yin Zhen is the true, original white tea from the local subvarieties of *Camellia sinensis* var. *sinensis* that produce particularly large, succulent buds. Beware non-Fujianese bud white teas called "Silver Needles" that are now being produced in other regions of China, Sri Lanka, and other tea-producing countries. While these teas may be tasty, they are not true Bai Hao Yin Zhen.

BAI MUDAN (White Peony)

REGION: Fujian Province, China (and many other locations worldwide)

MANUFACTURE: Air-dried white tea (ranges from 5 to 12 percent oxidation); may require a period of finish-fire bake-drying

STYLE: Open leaf, usually blended with varying percentages of buds

FLAVOR: Soft, with a hint of black tea's taste

AROMA: Fresh, with notes of clean clay

LIQUOR: Pale straw to light amber color

STEEPING: Numerous 2- to 3-minute infusions at 160° to 170°F. Drink plain.

This modern-style white tea is made from China bush if sourced from a Chinese garden, and from China or Assam bush if sourced from another country. Perfectly good and tasty tea, Bai Mudan is an inexpensive and delicious light tea. Bai Mudan was developed in response to the high demand for leaf processed as white tea without the specific pluck demands and subsequent high price of the original white tea, Bai Hao Yin Zhen. The use of leaf pluck gives Bai Mudan a stronger flavor, which many tea drinkers prefer and which will provide better results if the tea is to be flavored.

WHITE TEA

Tips for Purchasing White Tea

The aroma of authentic Chinese white tea is delicate and subtle. When purchasing Bai Hao Yin Zhen, look closely at the buds. The tea should consist of long, uniform, slender, spear-shaped buds that are covered with downy, silvery-white hairs. The overall appearance should be elegant and distinguished. The buds should have a soft, matte appearance, and the best grades have a slight greenish luster. Bai Hao Yin Zhen has been described as "white as the clouds, pure as the snow, aromatic as an orchid, and green as the fields." In the best of years the production of authentic Fujian Bai Hao Yin Zhen white tea is small, so this tea has always been desirable and costly.

Bai Mudan is less pretty, but there is a production standard that the appearance should exemplify. Bai Mudan leaf will not be shaped into fanciful twists, curls, and so on as the leaf is for green tea; it is either air-dried or simply fired in a drying oven (not in a tea-firing pan or basket). This means that the tea will be light, fluffy, and voluminous. Silvery buds (plucked later than the buds used to make Bai Hao Yin Zhen) are easily spotted in the mix.

Two other delicious white teas are also made in Fujian: the leafy Gong Mei and Shou Mei. Anhui and Zhejiang Provinces both scent silver needle-style white tea with fresh jasmine blossoms and call it Silver Needles with Jasmine. Because leaf white teas undergo even more withering than Bai Hao Yin Zhen does (which encourages significant oxidation), the appearance of modern-style leaf white tea will vary in color as well as particle composition. This leaf will feature a mix of shades, such as army green, light green, greenish light gray, and honey. The leaf should not be all one color.

The Perfect Cup: Specifics for Steeping White Tea

The delicacy of white tea can easily be rendered harsh if the tea is scorched with water that is too hot. Treat white tea more like green tea than oolong or black tea, by steeping it in water that has boiled and cooled (or that was only heated to the proper temperature).

Because of the light, fluffy nature of modern-style white tea, it is important to use enough leaf to have the proper flavor in the cup. Similar to the measure of other large-leaf, voluminous teas (such as Wu Yi Shan rock oolongs and Tai Ping Hou Kui green tea), we measure leafy white tea in tablespoons and bud white tea in teaspoons. White teas are good candidates for multiple steepings; try using a slightly hotter water temperature each time and increase the steeping time for each re-infusion.

The following measurements will work whether you are using a *gaiwan*, an individual teacup or mug, or a teapot, and can be scaled up directly. When you become familiar with a tea, adjust to your taste.

MEASUREMENT	WATER TEMPERATURE
2 tablespoons for leafy tea; 2 teaspoons for bud tea (per 6 ounces of water)	160° to 170°F

STEEPING TIME	NUMBER OF STEEPINGS
90 seconds to 2 minutes	One to three

WHITE TEA

Major Tea-Producing Countries and Regions: White Tea

The Role of White Tea

As is true for all the "original" classes of tea produced by and perfected in a certain place in the world, the manufacture of traditional white tea is not simply a matter of learned production skills that can be applied to tea buds in any location. Authentic white tea is a perfect example of *terroir* and the skills of the tea workers that conspire to give it a consistent, recognizable flavor.

Today, in certain regions of China (Anhui, Yunnan) and in India (Assam, Darjeeling, Nilgiri), Sri Lanka, and the Himalaya, tea growers produce their own versions of "silver needles" and leafy "white" teas. Many of these teas are exquisite in appearance and represent skillful bud pluck and manufacture, but we find many of them to be lacking in flavor (or just plain odd) compared to the Fujianese original. At best, they must be different than the original, and when honestly presented can be quite delicious.

White teas made outside of China are being produced primarily to capture some of the growing demand by tea companies for inexpensive leafy white tea for use in flavored white-tea blends and for making RTD (Ready-to-Drink) bottled tea beverages. They are not the same as the traditional, authentic white teas from Fujian Province, China.

Authentic white tea is produced in three restricted locales in northeast Fujian Province, China: Fuding County, Jianyang County, and Zhenghe County. While many tea bushes are plucked for leaf used to make white tea, five main tea bush varieties are cultivated for the production of traditional, authentic white tea. The leaves of these tea plants are broad and large and uniquely able to produce large buds that maintain a covering of fine, downy white hair after processing. These tea bush cultivars are:

- Fuding Da Bai (Fuding Big White)
- Fuding Da Hao (Fuding Big Sprout)
- Zhenghe Da Bai (Zhenghe Big White)
- Zhenghe Da Hao (Zhenghe Big Sprout)
- Xiao Bai (Small White)

Plucking Style for White Tea

The pluck and manufacture for white tea in Fujian Province, China, are:

- Bai Hao Yin Zhen (Silver Needles): Plucked from the tender spring buds of the Fuding Da Bai, Fuding Da Hao, Zhenghe Da Bai, and Zhenghe Da Hao tea bushes.
- Bai Mudan (White Peony): The highest grades (there are six grades in total) are a blend of the first two full leaves and a percentage of buds that are left after the production of Bai Hao Yin Zhen. The higher the percentage of buds, the better the grade of Bai Mudan. Made from both Fuding Da Bai and Zhenghe Da Bai tea bushes.
- Gong Mei (Tribute Eyebrow): Made after the production of Bai Hao Yin Zhen and Bai Mudan, Gong Mei is manufactured from the large leaves of the Xiao Bai tea bush cultivar.

- Shou Mei (Long Life Eyebrow): Similar to Gong Mei, but the pluck is a grouping of three or four large leaves. Shou Mei white tea is made from the Fuding Da Hao tea bush cultivars and is especially popular in Hong Kong tea houses. On rare occasions buds can be added to Shou Mei if a tea merchant requests it, and the fresh leaf is also used to make a Fujianese version of Bai Hao oolong tea.

Blooming flower teas are sometimes made with white tea buds, as are several high-quality, fresh-blossom jasmine-scented teas, such as Silver Needles with Jasmine and Yin Hao Jasmine.

The Harvest Year: Seasonal Plucks for White Tea

White teas are made from early spring to late spring. Buds for Bai Hao Yin Zhen are plucked in the earliest days of spring and are the first white teas made. The plucking schedule for Yin Zhen is only a few days each year that begin and end before March 15. Yin Zhen must be plucked on a day when there is no rain or dew present on the plants in the early morning, and the condition of the buds must be flawless. The Bai Mudan pluck begins after the Bai Hao Yin Zhen is finished, so it usually begins by March 15 and ends about April 10. The Bai Mudan plucking standard for the condition of the leaf and buds is very high.

As the days pass and the buds and leaves grow larger, production of Gong Mei and Shou Mei white teas commence. White tea production in Fujian is usually finished by the middle of May.

Leaf Manufacture: Production Methods for White Tea

White teas are often discussed as though they are a type of green tea, but this is not true. In fact, the production techniques for white tea and green tea are completely different. Whereas green teas are de-enzymed and fired to control moisture content and prevent oxidation, white tea is not de-enzymed.

After the pluck, white tea manufacture utilizes two critical steps that are essential to black tea manufacture: **withering**, both outdoor (solar) and indoor on bamboo mats, and **bake-drying**.

Bai Hao Yin Zhen is withered and slowly dried in order to preserve the shape of the bud and the downy plant hairs. Modern-style white teas are also allowed to dry slowly into a natural, bulky shape, in contrast to green tea, which is shaped by hand or by machine into curls, twists, balls, needles, and so on.

Simple, no-shape drying results in teas that are light, fluffy, and multihued. In the cup, one can taste the influence of the wither on the flavor. The flavor of white tea is not as sweet or astringent as a green tea's variously can be, nor does it have the vegetal flavors often associated with green tea. Rather, white tea is soft and rich, with subdued aromas and flavors that suggest honey, chestnuts, toast, apricots, and brown rice.

All white teas have an undercurrent of flavor that is faintly reminiscent of a light black tea, such as a Nilgiri or Nepal. The color of modern-style white tea's liquor ranges from pale orange to copper, while Bai Hao Yin Zhen infuses to a pale honey color. In each case, the color is a reflection of the unique processing of the fresh bud or leaf plant material.

WHITE TEA

OOLONG TEA

In China and Taiwan, oolong teas are highly revered. Westerners who can negotiate their way knowledgeably around this very alluring and rewarding class of tea are deemed to possess a high degree of tea sophistication.

Oolong tea offers tea enthusiasts a wide-ranging choice of styles, aromas, and flavors. As a group these teas are gloriously diverse, with a unique set of particulars regarding leaf style, color, oxidation level, and degree of roasting. But because there is much diversity in where and how these teas are made, and because of the overall complexity of oolong tea, each tea enjoys character traits that afford them individuality within their larger group.

In traditional Chinese tea shops oolong tea is sold as "wulong" or "black dragon" tea, aptly named for the long, heavily fired leaves of dark, traditional strip-style oolong teas. Perhaps this tea is so named because its appearance resembles the twisting silhouette of the mystical Chinese dragon, which suggests authority and nobility.

Chinese and Taiwanese tea experts say that Pu-erh tea is the most complicated tea to study and learn (but relatively straightforward to manufacture), but that oolong tea is the most intricate and complex tea to manufacture. This is due to the fact that oolong teas are partially oxidized and can be made within a range of 12 to 80 percent oxidation that will vary with the type of oolong tea being manufactured.

To put these percentages into perspective, green tea has zero oxidation, and black tea is 100 percent oxidized. This difference encompasses a big swing, and within it lies all of the complexity, nuance, and enticing flavor and aroma that has made oolong tea so enduringly popular.

In some ways oolong tea is a composite of all tea, incorporating many of the fine points of all other classes of tea with additional steps and techniques that are unique to oolong manufacture. Production time for oolong tea can be as long as thirty-six to forty hours, making these teas both labor-intensive and challenging for tea makers. The reward for this work is strikingly flavorful tea with aromas that are redolent of melons, apricots, honey, leather, wood, spice, and orchids.

The flavor of oolong tea is complex, and each tea relies on the skills of the tea maker to capture the true essence of the variety of tea bush or tea tree in the taste of the tea. Oolong tea producers are proud to say that while their teas may not be showy on the outside (as is the case with many artisan green teas), the flavor goodness lies within the tea leaves, where it awaits its release with water.

There are three broad categories of oolong tea from China and Taiwan: open leaf–style, semiball-rolled–style, and strip-style.

Open Leaf–Style Oolongs

Open leaf–style oolongs, such as Baozhong and Bai Hao Oriental Beauty, are unique to Taiwan and are easily identified by their open, slightly curled, leafy appearance and pure, sweet refreshing aromas and flavors. Baozhong has a luxurious

OOLONG TEA

flavor with a strong emphasis on fresh, youthful, springtime aromas; Bai Hao has a deeper, mellower flavor and the aroma is reminiscent of chestnuts and apricots. These teas are easily recognizable by the following characteristics:

- Medium to large, slightly crimped leaves
- Light oxidation (Baozhong 12 to 18 percent) or medium oxidation (Bai Hao Oriental Beauty 65 to 75 percent)
- No roasting
- Pure, sweet, bright, distinctive flavors and aromas
- Colors that range from vibrant woodland green to a textured mixture of dark brown and chestnut brown leaf with the presence of white tip along the edges

Semiball-Rolled–Style Oolongs

Semiball-rolled oolongs, such as China's Ben Shan, Huang Jin Gui (Golden Osmanthus), Mao Xie (Hairy Crab), Tou Tian Xiang (Imperial Gold), and Tieguanyin, and Taiwan's Tieguanyin, Tung Ting, and various High Mountain gao shan oolongs are easily identified by their distinctive ball shape with attached pieces of stem. These oolongs are made in a traditional style and a modern style of oxidation.

SEMIBALL-ROLLED–STYLE WITH TRADITIONAL-STYLE OXIDATION

This is the favorite style of oolong among Chinese and Taiwanese tea drinkers. Characteristics include:

- Irregular-shaped balls of tea with varying amounts of stem attached to the leaf
- Medium oxidation (35 to 65 percent) that varies with each specific type of tea and tea maker
- Medium roasting, which encourages a honey, stone-fruit taste and aroma
- Mottled color, ranging from a light amber-brown to slightly reddish, chestnut brown

SEMIBALL-ROLLED-STYLE WITH MODERN-STYLE OXIDATION

Similar in appearance to the traditional, roasted versions, modern-style oolongs are green in color and consist of slightly larger, less compacted balls of tea. This style of oolong tea has become quite popular in the West. Characteristics include:

- Irregular-shaped balls of tea with substantial amounts of stem attached to the leaf
- Light oxidation (25 to 40 percent) that varies with each tea and individual tea maker
- Light, minimal roasting to preserve floral flavor and fragrance or is not roasted
- Mottled color, ranging from gold-green to rich forest green or soft, jade green

Strip-Style Oolongs

Strip-style oolongs, such as Wu Yi Shan rock oolongs and Feng Huang Dan Congs, are unique to China. These teas are easy to identify because of their distinctive leaf characteristics and their dark color, which suggests that the leaf has been highly oxidized and roasted. Characteristics include:

- Full, long, large, slightly twisted individual leaves without stem
- Varying oxidation (50 to 80 percent)
- Heavy roasting, which enhances flavor, deepens color, and adds warmth and strength
- Strong, fruity flavors and earthy, pervasive, and lingering aromatics
- Monotone colors, ranging from deep forest brown to dark, flinty gray-black

Classic Leaf Styles (Shapes) of Manufactured Oolong Tea (Dry Leaf)

- Open or leafy
- Strip-style
- Ball-rolled

Oolong Tea Flavor (Taste) Components

Oolong teas have a great range of taste profile because their oxidation can vary from 20 to 80 percent, the base leaf can be from so many different subvarieties of *Camellia sinensis*, and oolongs are traditionally infused many times.

- Aromatic
- Body—full
- Brisk
- Character
- Earthy
- Full
- Herbaceous
- Lingering finish
- Smooth
- Soft
- Stone fruit
- Sweet

Gallery of Oolong Teas

BAI HAO (Oriental Beauty)

REGION: Beipu Township, Hsinchu County, Taiwan

MANUFACTURE: 65 to 75 percent oxidation

STYLE: Open-twist, folded-leaf

FLAVOR: Sweet, fresh, "honeyed" fruit

AROMA: Pure and clean fragrance of apricots and peaches

LIQUOR: Clear, pale golden color

STEEPING: Numerous 3- to 4-minute infusions at 180° to 195°F
(increasing temperature with the steepings). Drink plain.

Bai Hao is Taiwan's premier oolong and most famous tea, and it is referred to by various names in English. It is easy to drink and delicious and has a very short, summer-only harvest season. A traditional, leafy oolong, Bai Hao has the characteristic stone-fruit flavor and aroma that makes it an excellent and indulgent "sipping" tea. Bai Hao oolong can be enjoyed with food—especially sweet or slightly savory snacks. Serve in small porcelain cups with a light-colored, unpatterned interior. A properly prepared Bai Hao oolong will present a remarkable aroma and clean taste.

BAOZHONG

REGION: Pinglin and Wenshan Townships, Taipei County, Taiwan

MANUFACTURE: 12 to 18 percent oxidation; oven-fired and roasted

STYLE: Long, open-twist leaf, with few stems

FLAVOR: Creamy and rich, with no astringency

AROMA: Offers an enticing "pure tea" fragrance

LIQUOR: Delicate, pale gold color

STEEPING: Numerous 3- to 4-minute infusions at 180° to 190°F
(increasing temperature with the steepings). Drink plain.

This tea is a specialty of Taiwan's premier tea gardens in Pinglin township, Taipei County, home to the Taiwan Pinglin Tea Industry Museum and educational center.

Baozhong is minimally processed. The leaf is long and slightly twisted due to gentle, minor handling, with the light color expected from nominal oxidation. The liquor is soft and sweet in style, with a delightful fresh aroma and elegant aftertaste. For tea enthusiasts who enjoy a subtle, clear, and refreshing beverage, Baozhong is a great choice. Locals in Taiwan say that the pale golden liquor is the clear color of a full moon.

OOLONG TEA

DA HONG PAO (Royal Red Robe)

REGION: Fujian Province, China

MANUFACTURE: 80 percent oxidation

STYLE: Strip-style, individual-leaf pluck

FLAVOR: Deep and rich, with a Scotchlike peatiness

AROMA: Dark and "earthy," it changes with the steepings

LIQUOR: Deeply golden to dark amber color

STEEPING: Three to six 30-second to 2-minute infusions at 185° to 200°F (increasing temperature with the steepings). Drink plain.

Da Hong Pao is characteristically highly oxidized; its leaf lies at the extreme end of the scale for oolong manufacture. At 80 percent oxidation it visually resembles a black tea, but the leaves are much larger than most black teas. The Da Hong Pao subvariety of tea bush is often pruned to a single trunk, and its leaves are among the largest leaf plucked for tea of any style. Leaf for each of the premium, traditional strip-style Wu Yi Shan oolongs is plucked from a particular subvariety of *Camellia sinensis* var. *sinensis*. Da Hong Pao is a perfect example of this distinctive relationship of subvariety of tea bush and its leaf to a finished oolong tea.

FENG HUANG DAN CONG
"ZHI LAN XIANG" ("Orchid Fragrance")

REGION: Guangdong Province, China

MANUFACTURE: 70 to 80 percent oxidation

STYLE: Strip-style, individual-leaf pluck

FLAVOR: Intricate layers of complex flavor (similar to the profile of a single-malt Scotch)

AROMA: Sweet and intense, with multilayered floral notes

LIQUOR: Amber-orange, tinged with a silver hue

STEEPING: Three to six 30-second to 2-minute infusions at 180° to 200°F (increasing temperature with the steepings). Drink plain.

Dan Congs bear a similarity to the strip-style Wu Yi Shan oolongs in style and appearance. Finely focused and exquisitely floral, the best Dan Congs are unique in the tea world. Unlike Wu Yi Shan oolongs, which are plucked from specific old tea bushes, Dan Cong teas are plucked from specific strains of old tea trees. Each tree and its resulting tea is called a "fragrance," so named for the striking flavor and aroma characteristics each tea evokes. Feng Huang Dan Congs are less austere in style than the yan cha oolongs from Wu Yi, but make no mistake, these teas are substantial in flavor.

OOLONG TEA

TIEGUANYIN (Wild-Grown Anxi or "Monkey-Picked")

REGION: Min-Nan region (south of the Min River), Fujian Province, China

MANUFACTURE: 25 to 40 percent oxidation; traditionally charcoal-fired

STYLE: Semiball-rolled with attached stems

FLAVOR: Deep and richly sweet

AROMA: Very fresh, stone-fruit fragrance

LIQUOR: Golden amber

STEEPING: Numerous 30-second to 2-minute infusions at 185° to 195°F (increasing temperature with the steepings). Drink plain.

Wild-grown, or "monkey-picked," oolong is a reference to the difficult-to-reach places on which these indigenous, traditional-style Tieguanyin tea bushes flourish.

Tieguanyin should be steeped repeatedly, each for a brief time. The infusions will vary, initially being light and clear, then becoming very rich and mouth-filling, finally returning to an aromatic, clear liquor. The leaves will swell and open gradually until the full leaf is exposed, showing off the lovely crimson-tinged edge of the leaf. This demonstrates the tea artisans' expertise during the bruising and rattling step of leaf manufacture.

TUNG TING

REGION: Lugu Township, Nantou County, Taiwan

MANUFACTURE: 40 to 50 percent oxidation; charcoal-fired

STYLE: Semiball-rolled with few or no stems

FLAVOR: Smooth, nutty, and sweet

AROMA: Clean, intensely caramel-nut

LIQUOR: Golden green-yellow

STEEPING: Numerous 30-second to 2-minute infusions at 180° to 190°F (increasing temperature with the steepings). Drink plain.

Nantou County in Taiwan is the home of Tung Ting, sometimes spelled Dong Ding. Tung Ting offers complex aromatics, lush mouthfeel, and varying flavors throughout multiple infusions. The best Tung Ting oolongs are hand-processed from gardens located in the highest reaches of Tung Ting Mountain, where it is known as "frozen-peak" tea. It is one of the most highly regarded oolongs, commanding a premium price because of high demand worldwide. Traditionally steeped in a *gaiwan*, Tung Ting explodes with a nutty, caramel, and chestnut aroma and flavor that is refreshing and invigorating.

OOLONG TEA

Tips for Purchasing Oolong Tea

The following list details some of the information you may encounter (with more or less specificity, depending on the source) when purchasing oolong tea:

1. The country of origin
   Ex: China or Taiwan
2. The specific region of China
   Ex: Fujian Province or Guangdong Province
3. The specific mountain and county in Taiwan
   Ex: Ali Shan, Jiayi County or Tung Ting, Nantou County
4. Specific style of oolong
   Ex: semiball-rolled or strip-style
5. Tea bush subvariety
   Ex: Shui Xian or Tieguanyin
6. Year of harvest
7. Season of the pluck
   Ex: spring, summer, fall, winter (Taiwan only)
8. Plucking style
   Ex: hand-plucked or machine-sheared
9. Oxidation level
   Ex: the range is 25 to 80 percent in China and 12 to 75 percent in Taiwan
10. Level of roasting
    Ex: none, light, medium, heavy

The Perfect Cup: Specifics for Steeping Oolong Tea

Some oolong teas, such as semiball-rolled Tieguanyin and High Mountain gao shan oolongs, are ready for drinking as soon as they are made; nevertheless, some oolong tea enthusiasts prefer to allow their tea to rest and mellow before drinking. With the exception of Baozhong, oolongs are not subject to the time-sensitive requirements that green, yellow, and white teas are, nor must they be aged, as sheng Pu-erh is, before the best flavor develops.

In China, oolongs are steeped in an unglazed clay teapot or a *gaiwan*, both of which are perfect vessels for the way that these teas are best steeped. Oolongs yield more multiple infusions than any other class of tea except Pu-erh. Because of this, one must put more oolong leaf into an unglazed clay teapot or *gaiwan* than one would use when steeping green, yellow, white, or black tea.

The following measurements are for steeping oolong teas Asian style. (For Western-style steeping, use two teaspoons to one tablespoon of tea [two to three grams] per six ounces of water and adjust the quantity of leaf used by the size of the leaf. See chapter two for more details.)

MEASUREMENT	WATER TEMPERATURE
Begin with 2 to 3 tablespoons (5 to 6 grams) of tea (per 6 ounces of water)	180° to 200°F

STEEPING TIME	NUMBER OF STEEPINGS
First rinse the tea: place the tea into the teapot or *gaiwan*, add heated water, and swish it gently around the inside of the vessel. Quickly pour off this rinse water, and discard it. Add more water to steep the first infusion.	Four to eight or more, depending on the type of oolong tea and its age. Semiball-rolled–style oolongs hydrate more slowly than strip-style oolongs; aged versions of each hydrate more slowly again and have greater staying power, thus yield more steepings.

INFUSION TIMES	
Infusion Number	**Time**
First	10 seconds to 1 minute
Second	15 seconds to 65 seconds
Third and additional	Increase time by 5 to 10 seconds for each steeping, and as the flavor begins to diminish, add an additional 30 seconds for each remaining infusion. Steep at a slightly higher temperature for each successive infusion.

OOLONG TEA

Major Tea-Producing Countries and Regions: Oolong Tea

The Role of Oolong Tea

While oolong teas can be grouped into just three styles, the variations from place and method of manufacture combine to create a class of tea that could keep tea enthusiasts happily drinking and studying oolongs for a lifetime.

OOLONG TEA IN CHINA

China is the original home of oolong tea. Both Fujian and Guangdong Provinces, situated along China's southeast coast, produce China's extraordinary oolongs.

Fujian Province

Fujian Province is a treasure trove of spectacular tea, including traditional jasmine tea; traditional Bai Hao Yin Zhen and modern-style white tea; smoky Lapsang Souchong; and the historic but little-known Panyang Congou (Golden Monkey) family of black tea. Despite this bounty of significant tea, the most fascinating and notable teas in Fujian Province may well indeed be its glorious oolongs.

In northern Fujian, Wu Yi Shan strip-style oolong teas (known as rock or cliff teas) are time-honored. The Wu Yi Shan area is a spectacular natural landscape of rivers, bamboo forests, and classical limestone cliffs and peaks. This environment supports indigenous, varietal tea bushes that grow in the thin soil and mineral-rich crumbling rock shards along the cliffs and ridges. Tea grown within the highest cliff areas of the Wu Yi Shan is among the most cherished and expensive tea found in China's treasure chest of exceptional teas. The Wu Yi Shan is home to a collection of tea bush varieties that is unique in the world: the most prized tea bushes are those fifty years of age (and older!). The growth habit of tea bushes in the Wu Yi Shan is influenced by the rocky terrain of this rugged area—here tea bushes sprout from the ground in a sparse cluster of branches and produce only a small number of leaves per bush. Because the number of each of these old tea bush varietals is small and the collection of bushes as a whole is talked about in the same breath, these bushes are sometimes referred to as *single trunk* (or *single variety*) tea bush varieties. But make no mistake, despite their longevity and smaller yield, these bushes produce leaf that is some of China's most costly tea.

Of course, not all of the oolong tea produced in the Wu Yi Shan area is plucked from these old tea bushes: these teas are limited in availability, and the best of the best rarely leaves China. However, many new tea gardens have been established in lower elevation areas to supply the various levels of commercial-grade Wu Yi Shan teas that are prevelant in the marketplace. In addition to the age and location of the bushes, the relationship of the tea to the tea bush variety is important. Each tea is named after its particular tea bush variety. For example, while close to one hundred named subvarieties of tea bushes grow here, the four most famous Wu Yi Shan *yan cha* are plucked from only their specific tea bush varietals. These teas are:

- Da Hong Pao (Royal Red Robe)
- Bai Ji Guan (White Cockscomb)
- Tie Luo Han (Iron Arhat)
- Shui Jin Gui (Golden Water Turtle)

In southern Fujian Province, in the countryside surrounding the city of Anxi, heavily terraced tea gardens blend one into another and cover the mountainsides in a lush carpet of green. This region of Fujian is close to the coast and enjoys semitropical weather, providing a temperate climate for serious tea production. The soil here is rich and fertile (compared to the paucity of such in the Wu Yi Shan area) and red from an abundance of iron oxide.

In the Anxi area, oolong tea leaves undergo a unique rolling step during leaf manufacture. About midway through the manufacturing process, the leaves are placed in a cloth bag that is tied into a tight bundle and then placed in a machine that gently rolls (and slightly compresses) the bundles of tea in a circular manner for a prescribed amount of time. This rolling step (followed by tumbling the tea in a metal or bamboo tumbler) is how Anxi oolongs acquire their distinctive semiball-rolled shape.

Tieguanyin is made in twenty-seven villages in the Anxi region, and the fresh leaf is plucked primarily from the Red Heart and White Heart Guan Yin tea bush varieties. Other tea bush subvarieties in this area (known collectively as Se Zhong varieties) yield similar oolongs. A few examples are Ben Shan, Huang Jin Gui (Golden Osmanthus), Mao Xie (Hairy Crab), and Tou Tian Xiang (Imperial Gold).

Guangdong Province

In the northeast region of Guangdong Province the landscape features mountains, valleys, and streams. The five connecting peaks of the Phoenix Mountain range are in the vicinity of Chaozhou city. These mountains are famous for a unique oolong that rivals Wu Yi Shan rock oolong teas (*yan cha*) in distinction and finesse: Feng Huang Dan Cong.

Whereas *yan cha* is plucked from single-variety old tea bushes, the best Feng Huang Dan Cong is plucked from much larger single-variety old tea trees. The most important Feng Huang Dan Cong teas are plucked from old, wild-growing, large-leaf arbor tea trees that are found in the high reaches (above 4,260 feet) of the Phoenix Mountains. Over the centuries, these tea plants have grown into stately old tea trees which reach heights of twelve to fifteen feet. The structural habit of these old tea trees can vary: some have branches that split from a main trunk inches off the ground while others sprout from the ground in a sparse cluster of two, three, or a small handful of branches. And in some cases, old trees have been pruned like a tree with one central trunk.

These old trees have produced offspring trees, and those trees too have reproduced another generation. The younger trees have been planted at lower elevations, so as with Wu Yi Shan teas, all the Feng Huang Dan Cong tea does not come from the old tea trees. Lower elevation trees produce the majority of commercial Feng Huang Dan Cong oolong. Some of these lower elevation tea trees were planted roughly fifty years ago; others are much younger.

The old tea tree varieties have individual characteristics, growth habits, shapes, and flavor/aroma profiles, and the tea is named for its specific tea tree variety. Collectively, these tree varieties are referred to as the "fragrances" and are recognized by distinguished names, such as:

- Rou Gui Xiang (Cinnamon Fragrance)
- Xing Ren Xiang (Almond Fragrance)
- Zhi Lan Xiang (Orchid Fragrance)

Finished Feng Huang Dan Congs are similar in appearance to Wu Yi Shan rock oolongs, and are made from individually plucked, large, sturdy fresh leaves. The tea leaves are dark in color, long, and slightly thick in appearance, with a slight twist. The roast style is heavy; and in the cup, the liquor resonates with chewy body; deep fruity flavors; and full, rich fragrance. As with *yan cha*, there is a universe of tantalizing flavor and strikingly exotic perfumed fragrance in each variety of Feng Huang Dan Cong.

OOLONG TEA IN TAIWAN

The heritage of Taiwan's glorious oolongs harkens back to Fujian Province, China, and the tea-manufacturing skills and tea bush cuttings that arrived in Taiwan with migrating Fujianese immigrants in the mid-nineteenth century.

Naturally, today there is a similarity between some of these oolongs.

But Taiwan oolongs are distinctly Taiwanese in nature; only a few sips are necessary to appreciate these spectacular teas that uniquely express the *terroir* and tea-making style of Taiwan. Despite the confines of this small island country, Taiwan is blessed with a nearly perfect geographic location, abundant natural resources, and an ideal subtropical climate. Tea farmers and producers use that to their advantage— Taiwan's oolongs are some of the world's most aromatic, expressive, expensive, and rare teas. Tawian oolongs include a larger span of leaf styles and oxidation levels than their Chinese oolong cousins, giving tea enthusiasts more delicious choices to explore.

Leaf-style Taiwan oolongs are easy to identify because of their open, slightly curled, leafy appearance and pure, sweet refreshing flavors. Some of these teas will age nicely, others not as well. Semiball-rolled modern-style oolongs are meant to be drunk young. These teas are elegant, sweet, and refreshing. They possess lovely floral aromas reminiscent of orchids and heady, exotic flowers. Semiball-rolled traditional-style oolongs are roasted to varying degrees. And much like their Chinese counterparts, roasted oolongs are earthy, mouth-filling, and well developed, with almost chewy body and aromas reminiscent of honey, peaches, and apricots. These teas can be drunk young or aged.

But perhaps the most intriguing Taiwanese teas are the High Mountain gao shan oolongs. These teas are those that grow at more than 6,000 feet; most tea gardens in Taiwan are located at 1,900 to 8,000 feet. The tea gardens in the high-mountain areas of Ali Shan, Li Shan, and Shan Lin Xi, in central Taiwan, are small, and the steep incline of the mountainside makes growing and plucking tea in this lush environment difficult work. The tea bushes yield relatively small quantities of astoundingly good tea, and the good news for the tea farmers is that their teas are in constant high demand by tea enthusiasts worldwide. The soil, weather, and dedication of artisan tea farmers and producers comes together to craft achingly lovely, intensely floral teas.

Additionally, High Mountain gao shan oolongs possess bold and sweet flavors that are direct, pure, and heavily influenced by the minerality in the soil and the constant chill in the high-mountain air. The combination of high altitude and cool, thin air of the high-mountain tea gardens conspire to produce some of the most delicious teas on the planet. The best High Mountain gao shan teas are hand-plucked by small-scale tea farmers who take pride in their crop.

These teas do not have a standardized oxidation level, because most tea processors do it by eye and from experience: they know when their tea is at its glorious best. But these teas are always semiball-rolled, and the choicest ones have significant bits of stem attached to the leaves. A well-made, hand-plucked High Mountain gao shan will unfurl to reveal what was plucked: a stem cluster with as many as four connected leaves. These teas are as magnificent to look at as they are to drink. Their vibrant, jade-green hues nearly sparkle, and the individual rolled balls can be quite large and impressive in appearance. These teas possess sweet, refreshing, vivacious flavors and persistent, vegetal aromas. Despite their high cost, many High Mountain gao shan teas never leave Taiwan, as they are spoken for year after year by Taiwanese customers loyal to these artisan farmers.

Elsewhere across the island, the number of cultivars growing in various pockets of Taiwan is estimated to number somewhere between fifty and one hundred. Skilled tea makers use the cultivars that their experience tells them will make the best tea. The most widely planted cultivars in Taiwan are known by several names:

- Chin Sin (green centered)
- Chin Sin Dapan (soft centered)
- Jin Xuan (Tai Cha #12, 27 son)
- Tsui-Yu (Tai Cha #13, 29 son)
- Si Ji (Evergreen 4 Season)

The tea bush cultivar is important in Taiwan, but outside of Taiwan, tea is primarily sold by the leaf style, amount of oxidation, and style of roasting, rather than by the region where the tea was produced. It is only recently that some Western tea merchants have begun listing the name of the cultivar with the tea.

Plucking Style for Oolong Tea

The fresh leaf plucked for oolong tea is larger than for other classes of tea, and the pluck is generally comprised of one to four leaves. An entire leaf set is plucked and used for semiball-rolled oolongs, but separate leaves are plucked for open, leafy oolongs and strip-style oolongs.

PLUCKING STYLE IN CHINA

In China, all tea is made from hand-plucked leaf. For Wu Yi Shan rock oolong tea the plucking standard is three or four separately plucked leaves (the fourth leaf is removed during

Tea in Honor of a Female Buddhist Deity

The Buddhist deity Guan Yin is known in China as the Goddess of Mercy. This beloved deity was introduced to China from India in the first century as the male god Avalokitesvara; over the centuries he was slowly transformed into a female by practitioners of Chinese Buddhism. The tea we know as Tieguanyin was named in honor of Guan Yin, and it is produced in both Fujian Province and Taiwan. The tea bush varietal for Tieguanyin differs from other semiball-rolled oolong teas in several ways. The fresh leaf is both strong and yielding at the same time. It is thick and requires more kneading and twisting in the processing than the fresh leaf from other semiball-rolled–style oolong varietals. The fresh leaf undergoes a slower oxidation and a long processing time, factors that contribute to the soft, apricots-and-peaches character of Tieguanyin. Tieguanyin oolong continues to be roasted in the old tradition.

the sorting of the leaf and is reserved for less expensive grades of Wu Yi Shan oolongs and in blends). The leaves are not connected, and they are processed individually.

Tieguanyin producers require a pluck that is a small leaf cluster of two or three leaves still connected to the stem. The highest grades of early-season plucked tea are sold singly; lower grades and later plucks are used in blends. Tieguanyin is plucked entirely by hand; other oolongs in this region can be cut using a hand sickle.

To make Feng Huang Dan Cong teas, individual large leaves are plucked. The leaves are not connected and are processed individually.

PLUCKING STYLE IN TAIWAN

In Taiwan, leaf is both hand-plucked and machine-sheared in the lower elevation areas and hand-plucked in the tea gardens that produce High Mountain gao shan tea. Hand-plucked oolongs are more costly and more choice because each pluck of fresh leaf is a more complete unit of leaf and stem.

The Harvest Year: Seasonal Plucks for Oolong Tea

Despite a several-season plucking schedule, the best oolongs are made from the spring and the fall harvests in China and the spring and winter harvests in Taiwan.

SEASONAL PLUCKS IN CHINA

Leaf plucking for oolong tea begins a little later than the plucking schedule for most other Chinese teas. For all oolong leaf (but especially for the larger leaves of the old tea bushes and old tea trees) more time is needed after bud-break for their leaves to grow to the proper size.

Wu Yi Shan Rock Oolong

These teas are plucked only once a year in the spring, usually for a five- to ten-day period that falls between mid-April and early May. For commercial-grade Wu Yi Shan rock oolong teas, the plucking cycle begins in April with a first plucking, then a second plucking in May, a third plucking in June, a fourth plucking in September (has the best fragrance), and a fifth plucking at the end of October to early November (winter pluck).

Tieguanyin and Se Zong Oolong

These teas roughly follow the same plucking schedule as the commercial-grade Wu Yi Shan rock oolongs.

Feng Huang Dan Cong Oolong

The oldest tea trees are only plucked once a year in the spring. For young tea trees producing commercial-grade tea, five plucks per year are possible, but the best seasons are spring for flavor and fall for aroma.

SEASONAL PLUCKS IN TAIWAN

Taiwan boasts such a diversity of elevations, weather patterns, and seasonality that it is hard to discuss a uniform schedule for yearly plucking. In general, the growing season follows the general pattern of most tea countries, with the exception of a winter pluck, which is one of the year's best where it occurs.

Late spring and early summer yield teas with bright flavor and flowery fragrance. In late summer and early fall, higher temperatures result in yields with more leaf, but they are less distinctive teas. The cooler weather of fall and early winter brings a return of flavor and aroma to the plucks. The most concentrated flavors and aroma and long aftertaste are from the winter to early spring plucks.

Leaf Manufacture: Production Methods for Oolong Tea

The three most important steps in oolong manufacture are:

1. Repeated solar and indoor withering
2. Tossing and bruising the leaf (bruising the edges of the leaf encourages oxidation to begin)
3. Resting the leaf in between the repeated tossing and bruising

These tossing and bruising steps are unique to oolong manufacture and are repeated several times, depending on the region and the type of oolong being made.

Oolongs are made to a certain stable point, at which they are called *primary tea.* Primary tea can be held at this stage until it is time for the "refining," or finishing, process.

Refining deepens the flavor of the tea and brings out character. It enhances the staying power of the tea and allows it to be successfully reinfused additional times. Refining also adjusts the sweetness and aftertaste and reduces the moisture to a final, stable 5 percent.

OOLONG TEA PRODUCTION METHODS IN CHINA

The most complicated tea manufacture is oolong. While green tea can be made in one day, oolongs, properly and carefully made, can take as many as four days to be completed.

Strip-Style: Feng Huang Dan Cong and Wu Yi Shan Rock Oolongs

Traditional Wu Yi Shan rock oolong teas are made entirely by hand. While similar in process to that used to make Feng Huang Dan Cong teas, the best rock oolongs are not made using a cylinder roller or a mechanical dryer. Instead, the tea leaves are put into a tea-firing pan and de-enzymed. The leaf is taken quickly from the tea-firing pan and rolled and shaped by hand on a bamboo tray. This series of steps is repeated numerous times, as needed.

Finally, the tea is given a short roasting, which stabilizes the leaf until the second (final) roasting can be done. Final roasting is done in a bamboo basket over a low-ember charcoal fire that is covered with rice ash to ensure that no flame is present. Final roasting, like all aspects of a handmade tea, requires the skill and attention of a master roaster.

Feng Huang Dan Congs are given a long wither, three tossing-bruising-resting steps, vigorous rolling, a long oxidation period, and heavy roasting (longer firings at higher temperatures).

Semiball-Rolled–Style: Traditional-Style Oxidation Tieguanyin Oolongs

These teas require a light withering, rolling, oxidation, and roasting (shorter firings at lower temperatures) than Wu Yi Shan or Feng Huang Dan Cong oolongs. There are eighteen steps necessary to manufacture Tieguanyin oolong tea.

OOLONG TEA PRODUCTION METHODS IN TAIWAN

Taiwan oolongs are a great example of the old saying, "What is done in the processing to the fresh leaf is going to show up in the cup." In Taiwan, the choicest, hand-processed, semiball-rolled oolong teas command high prices. This is due to the fact that the tea processors who roll their leaf by hand do so many more times than leaf that is machine-rolled, and the monetary return they receive for their tea repays their efforts. High Mountain gao shan oolongs yield the smallest quantities year-round, but more attention is paid to the tea, and may be hand-rolled as many as forty different times. How many times a tea is rolled (plus other "trade secrets") contribute to the uniqueness of Taiwan's small tea farmer production.

Hand-rolling not only shapes the fresh leaf but also the gentle pressing on the fresh leaf releases the plant's internal juice and distributes it evenly over the surface of the leaf. This results in less clumping and more well-defined pellets of tea.

Firing, Roasting, and Aging Oolong Tea

As with all tea, oolongs are stabilized and fully fired before being sold. Firing is a lengthier process for oolong tea than for green tea, and must be carefully attended to. Oolong tea that is not properly fired will contain too much residual moisture and will spoil.

Roasting is an essential part of oolong tea production and much discussed in Asia. Roasting also adds complexity and richness to the flavor of the tea, and smoothes out the taste by softening the rough edges. A skilled tea roaster will fire the leaf on and off a smokeless charcoal fire for varying amounts of time until a light, medium, or heavy roasting is achieved. Roasting imparts varying degrees of color to the tea, from light brown to the rich, dark browns suggestive of cognac or a cigar.

Modern-style oolongs and Taiwanese High Mountain gao shan are roasted only lightly or sometimes not at all. The degree of roasting must be in sync with the oxidation level of the tea, so that one does not overwhelm the other, and the two facets of technique work together to yield a harmonious flavor. An oolong that is improperly roasted will lack fragrance, and fragrance is essential to oolong teas.

Once done, roasting cannot be undone. And heavy roasting should never be an attempt to give "character" to a tea that does not have it to begin with. Roasted oolongs are highly desirable, not just for what this step adds to the flavor of the tea but also for the ability of the tea to age into something wonderful and distinctive. Asian tea enthusiasts prize aged teas, and there is a long history of appreciation for tea that ages well. Modern-style oolongs, with little or no roasting, do not improve with age. (See chapter one for more on aged tea and chapter four for aging tea at home.)

OOLONG TEA

BLACK TEA

By the end of the Ming dynasty (1368–1644) tea drinking began to slowly take hold in the West. In the 1580s Portuguese traders brought tea from Japan to Europe. But tea did not find an appreciative audience until the Dutch embraced Chinese tea after 1640, when Dutch traders introduced tea to society patrons in The Hague and it became a fashionable rage.

Eventually, England entered the picture, and tea became the most sought-after trade commodity of the English East India Company. In fact, the English response to this mild-mannered beverage became a national obsession that was, over time, enjoyed by all citizens from royalty to the peasant class. Fully oxidized black tea became the favorite tea among European tea drinkers in general, a trend that remains true to this day.

Paradoxically, black tea is the least-consumed class of tea in China. This fact is a strange irony for China, which produces heavenly black teas. Black tea is not consumed to any large degree in Japan, Korea, or Taiwan, but it is the most widely consumed class of tea in India, Sri Lanka (formerly

known as Ceylon during the British colonial days), and the West. "Proper tea," as recognized by tea lovers in England, Ireland, Scotland, and parts of Europe, is strong black tea drunk with milk and sugar (sometimes copious amounts of both). In North America, black tea is the most popular for making both hot and iced tea, a taste preference that reflects the tea-drinking influence of England and Europe on our fledgling nations in the eighteenth century.

India and Sri Lanka, along with Kenya, produce the largest quantities of black tea. India and Sri Lanka have historically provided tea drinkers with four types of flavorsome and brisk teas:

- *Self-drinking tea:* Teas of singular character that can be drunk straight, without being blended
- *Single-estate tea:* The "single-malt Scotches" of the tea world—unblended, pure teas that are sourced from specific tea gardens and show all the characteristics of *terroir*, cultivation, plucking style, and manufacturing technique
- *Seasonal tea:* Teas made during a particular season
- *Blended tea:* Teas created by combining various teas from one country, such as Ceylon Morning Blend, or teas from several countries, such as English Breakfast Tea, Irish Breakfast Tea, and Russian Caravan. Blended teas are constructed for complexity of flavor and may (or may not) welcome the addition of milk and/or sugar. While these will not have the unique taste profile of the self-drinkers or single-estate teas, they may arguably be the best-drinking teas, due to the skill of the master blender at combining the best components of several teas into a perfect union.

BLACK TEA

Classic Leaf Styles (Shapes) of Manufactured Black Tea (Dry Leaf)

- Twist or curly
- Spiral or crimped
- Needle or wiry
- Ball or rolled
- Broken leaf
- CTC
- Granular
- Fannings

Black Tea Flavor (Taste) Components

The flavors that you elicit from black tea will vary with the method of steeping and the water used. Experiment!

- Aromatic
- Astringent
- Biscuity
- Body—varies from light to full
- Bold
- Brisk
- Character
- Colory
- Coppery
- Crisp
- Full
- Lingering finish
- Malty
- Nutty
- Point
- Short-finished
- Smoky
- Spicy
- Strength
- Sweet
- "Tea"

Gallery of Black Teas

CASTLETON GARDEN
1ST FLUSH FTGFOP1

REGION: Darjeeling, India

MANUFACTURE: Orthodox, with generous tip fired to a modern "green" style (see Glossary)

STYLE: Medium broken leaf, with light gold flecking

FLAVOR: Brisk, astringent, "muscatel"

AROMA: Pungent, with crisp, fresh notes

LIQUOR: Pale to medium gold color

STEEPING: 2 to 4 minutes at 180° to 195°F (or cooler). Check first-flush teas at 2 minutes and take note at what point a particular lot "bolts" (see below). Drink plain.

Darjeeling, the "Champagne of teas," is of the highest repute. First-flush Darjeelings are unusual in their briskness and have a peculiar flavor described as "muscatel," so Darjeeling tea is an acquired taste. We recommend tasting a Darjeeling every twenty to thirty seconds following the first two minutes of steeping, as a Darjeeling may "bolt" (see Glossary) all of a sudden, which contributes a distinctly sour sharpness that is rarely pleasant. Estates vary tremendously in style, finishing technique, and base tea subvariety: everything from straight China bush to Assam bush to local clonal (hybrid) varieties.

BLACK TEA

DIAN HONG (Golden Buds)

REGION: Yunnan Province, China

MANUFACTURE: Orthodox

STYLE: Full buds: open and flat, or curled into a spiral

FLAVOR: Smooth, rich, mouth-filling, caramel or honeylike

AROMA: Rich caramel and pear fragrance

LIQUOR: Clear, deeply golden color, tinged with an amber hue

STEEPING: 2 or 3 minutes at 180° to 190°F. (Bud-only black teas often can be short-steeped more than once—experiment!) Drink plain.

These full, long, and elegant buds yield a fantastic black tea with incredible depth of flavor and style, with nuances of honey and mouth-filling caramel. Dian Hongs may be straight and flat and called "Buds of Gold" or "Jumbo Golden Buds." The same pluck can be made slightly to tightly spiraled as Pan Long Yin Hao green tea would be, and is called "Golden Snail" or "Curly Golden Buds." They are extremely similar and unique in flavor among China black teas. Dian Hong in one form or another must be tasted at least once in a tea lifetime.

EVEREST HAND-ROLLED TIPS

REGION: Sindhupalchok District, Nepal

MANUFACTURE: Orthodox

STYLE: Large, needle budsets, hand-rolled artisan production

FLAVOR: Smooth, soft, and pleasant

AROMA: Bright and fresh

LIQUOR: Golden amber color, tinged with a copper hue

STEEPING: 3 to 5 minutes at 190° to 205°F. May be drunk plain or sweetened.

The large, hand-rolled budsets of this Nepalese black tea have the classic style of a Himalaya tea. Clean, crisp, and with a mouth-filling body that only a high altitude–grown tea can have, it is perfect for those who enjoy a black tea with little or no astringency and a full body. Nepal teas are grown at such high altitude that the growing season is brief, and the leaf does not have the ability to become harsh or bitter. Everest Hand-Rolled Tips is smooth, refreshing, and delicious, reflecting the high elevation of its origin.

BLACK TEA

GOOMTEE ESTATE 2ND FLUSH TGFOP

REGION: Darjeeling, India

MANUFACTURE: Orthodox, with minimal tip

STYLE: Medium broken flat, open leaf variegated with flashes of gold/green color

FLAVOR: Crisp, mineral, "muscatel"

AROMA: Sharply fresh and floral

LIQUOR: Bright copper color, tinged with an amber hue

STEEPING: 2 to 4 minutes at 190° to 205°F. Should be drunk plain, or as noted below.

This later pluck of further-matured leaf rounds out the classic "muscatel" Darjeeling flavor in the cup and tends toward a balance rarely offered by a first-flush Darjeeling.

Often showing a small percentage of "green" leaf (in the "German style"—see Glossary), modern Darjeeling teas are more intimidatingly sharp than their predecessors were, but the later plucks (second flushes and autumnals) of today's new clonals show less of this and may even tolerate the addition of milk. Darjeelings usually are not sweetened and do not accept citrus particularly well due to their inherent astringency.

KAMA BLACK FOP

REGION: Assam Valley, India

MANUFACTURE: Orthodox

STYLE: Large, whole-leaf; huge, crepey, single-leaf pluck

FLAVOR: Smooth, biscuity, robust, and malty

AROMA: Nutty and herbaceous

LIQUOR: Burnt sienna color, tinged with copper

STEEPING: 2 to 4 minutes at 190° to 205°F. (Superlarge-leaf black teas often can be short-steeped more than once—experiment!) Drink plain or with milk and/or sweetener.

This is the style of tea that true Assamese tea lovers drink. Huge intact leaves expertly plucked and processed are difficult to manufacture, and this leaf is a stunning example of the tea master's art. Seek out ultra-large-leaf Assam teas such as this for complex flavor. Put a few of these leaves in a small bowl and watch them unfurl as they breathe and stretch.

KEEMUN MAO FENG

REGION: Anhui Province, China

MANUFACTURE: Orthodox

STYLE: Long, thin, wiry budset tea

FLAVOR: Deep, rich

AROMA: Distinctively earthy, slightly reminiscent of chocolate

LIQUOR: Classic copper color

STEEPING: 3 to 5 minutes at 190° to 205°F. Drink plain or with milk and/
or sweetener.

Keemun teas are generally small-leafed, winey, crisp, and lean. Keemun Mao Feng, though, due to its larger-size pluck, is fatty and full-bodied. It has an unusual style and is as unique a black tea as one can find anywhere. One of the most distinctive flavor components that drinkers notice immediately is the unusual cocoalike dryness and chocolaty, lingering aftertaste. Keemun Mao Feng has none of the slight smokiness and charcoal-fired flavor that is classic to many Chinese black and oolongs teas, but rather mirrors the honeyed, clean, and clear, focused style of a premium large-leaf Assam or Ceylon tea.

KENILWORTH GARDEN OP

REGION: Kandy, Sri Lanka

MANUFACTURE: Orthodox, with minimal tip

STYLE: Large, twisted budset

FLAVOR: Deep, robust, and slightly biscuity

AROMA: Pure and clean

LIQUOR: Deeply burgundy-colored, tinged with a copper hue

STEEPING: 4 to 5 minutes at 190° to 205°F. Kenilworth Garden is best drunk plain but will take milk.

Teas from the Kandy tea-growing region of Sri Lanka are among the lesser-known but generally superhigh-quality Ceylon teas. Sitting on the border of Dimbula and Kandy, Kenilworth Garden offers the best qualities of these two world-class growing regions. It is exceptionally smooth, deeply satisfying, and full-bodied. Kenilworth Garden Ceylon tea will please the palate and offer a deeply liquored, thirst-quenching beverage with considerable lingering aftertaste. This is a beautiful self-drinking breakfast tea, or a calming, soft afternoon tea for those who enjoy their black tea "plain."

BLACK TEA

KOSABEI GARDEN FOP

REGION: Nandi Region, Kenya

MANUFACTURE: Orthodox, with significant tip

STYLE: Very large, twisted leaf

FLAVOR: Malty, brisk

AROMA: "Fresh" aroma is delicate but lingering

LIQUOR: Deep copper color

STEEPING: 3 to 5 minutes at 190° to 205°F. May be drunk plain, with milk and/or sweetener, and will show well with lemon.

Planted with Assam bush brought from India, the tea industry in Kenya has thrived due to the near-perfect growing conditions and dedication of the local "small-holder" tea farmers. Situated at the crossroads of the equator and the Great Rift Valley, the primary tea-growing areas of Kenya receive adequate moisture and plentiful sunshine that culminate in a year-round harvest with leaf being plucked every seventeen days in most areas. Fine orthodox Kenya tea will have considerable body with crisp astringency supplied by the tips. Kenya tea is consistently favorable in the cup whether manufactured to a CTC or an orthodox style.

LOVER'S LEAP ESTATE FOP

REGION: Nuwara Eliya, Sri Lanka

MANUFACTURE: Orthodox

STYLE: Large, whole-leaf, slighty crimped or twisted

FLAVOR: Brisk and structured, with point

AROMA: Clean and bright

LIQUOR: Golden amber color, tinged with a copper hue

STEEPING: 3 to 5 minutes at 185° to 200°F. Best drunk plain but will take milk or sweetener.

Nuwara Eliya gardens are among the finest Ceylon teas. Potentially lighter and brisker than their better-known cousins the Dimbulas, Nuwara Eliya teas are renown for their polish and finesse and are often accompanied by a brisk astringency. Sometimes referred to as the "Darjeelings of Ceylon," the best are made with a fairly large leaf, evenly graded into an open crimp or twist. In some years Nuwara Eliya teas can be a bit challenging to prepare properly; however, modest supervision during steeping returns a huge dividend in the incredible clarity and finesse of the cup.

PANYANG CONGOU (Golden Monkey)

REGION: Fujian Province, China

MANUFACTURE: Orthodox; may have significant tip

STYLE: Long, black budset, slightly twisted and tipped with gold

FLAVOR: Smooth, deep, and slightly malty

AROMA: Lingering, with wisps of earthiness

LIQUOR: Dark amber color, tinged with a copper hue

STEEPING: 3 to 5 minutes at 190° to 205°F. Panyang congou may be
drunk plain, with milk or citrus, and can be sweetened.

The Panyang congous of today have evolved from the "original" black tea that the Portuguese first brought back to Europe. "Golden Monkey" is a designation that can be used for many quality levels of this modern black tea, so when purchasing a Golden Monkey it is important to observe the leaf and purchase a small quantity first, in order to determine the style and particular flavor components of the one that you have found. A good Panyang congou should be complex and layered, and simply delicious with absolutely no astringency. The best ones are slightly more expensive than many other China black teas.

PARKSIDE SILVER FLAME

REGION: Nilgiri, India

MANUFACTURE: Orthodox, frost tea

STYLE: Bud-only, or can be a long, well-shaped budset

FLAVOR: Crisp, mineral

AROMA: Light, fresh, lingering

LIQUOR: Clear copper to pale amber color

STEEPING: 3 to 5 minutes at 185° to 195°F. (Bud-only and budset manufacture should allow multiple brief steepings.) May be drunk plain or with sweetener and/or lemon.

Teas from Tamil Nadu and Kerala in southern India's Blue Mountains (the Nilgiri) are sometimes known as "The Fragrant Ones." The winter harvest there is referred to as "frost tea." Most often consisting of a budset pluck, a frost tea has the clarity and freshness of a white tea, with the richness and lingering finish of a finely crafted black tea. A common trait is that teas produced in the Nilgiri tend to lack the amino acid that causes cloudiness in cold tea, so if you prefer your chilled tea "sparkling," this might be a good choice of leaf for preparing your iced tea.

TANZANIA CTC

REGION: Tanzania

MANUFACTURE: CTC (cut-tear-curl)

STYLE: Small granular particles

FLAVOR: Full, rich, malty

AROMA: Nutty, biscuity fragrance

LIQUOR: Burnt umber color, tinged with an orange hue

STEEPING: 3 to 5 minutes at 185° to 200°F. Drink plain or with milk or lemon and/or sweetener.

Most of the Tanzania tea manufactured today was developed from Assam bush plants grafted onto "native" Kenya rootstock. This gives the finished tea some of the maltiness of an Assam; however, the clarity of the Kenya style lightens and softens the whole. CTC-style tea comes in several size grades. Tanzania tea's particle size is in the moderate-size category, so the steeping methods are about the same as for a midsize broken-leaf orthodox tea. Consistently full-flavored and brisk, Tanzania tea is a favorite of tea drinkers who add milk or just prefer a deep, rich, satisfying cup.

ZHEN SHAN XIAO CHUNG
(Lapsang Souchong)

REGION: Fujian Province, China; and Taiwan

MANUFACTURE: Fully oxidized and smoked black tea

STYLE: Crepey, open twist leaf

FLAVOR: Biscuity, lightly to robustly smoked flavor

AROMA: Varying degrees of smokiness, over a bold, classic black tea fragrance

LIQUOR: Burnt sienna, tinged with a copper hue

STEEPING: Infuse 2 to 4 minutes at 190° to 210°F. Drink plain or with milk and/or sweetener.

When a large-leaf black tea is smoked over pine or other resinous wood, the result is this love-it-or-hate-it tea. Variation occurs due to the strength and inherent flavor profile of the base tea and the duration and intensity of the smoking. Both the standard market version and the original, authentic Lapsang Souchong are manufactured in unique smoking sheds located in the Zhen Shan of Fujian Province. To manufacture Lapsang Souchong, the smoking is part of the process of oxidizing the leaf into black tea. Excellent Lapsang Souchong is also manufactured in Taiwan, from the small amount of black tea produced there.

Tips for Purchasing Black Tea

There is no existing standard that governs how black teas should be labeled; each country has created its own set, so tea enthusiasts will find different pieces of information listed for tea from China than tea from India or Sri Lanka.

Depending on the vendor, a tea might have a great deal of information presented about it or detail could be lacking. The information may include:

1. The country of origin
   Ex: India or Sri Lanka
2. Specific region of origin
   Ex: Darjeeling or Dimbula
3. Name of the tea garden or estate
   Ex: Goomtee Estate
4. Year of the harvest
5. Season of the pluck
   Ex: spring, summer, fall, winter
6. The method of manufacture
   Ex: orthodox leaf or CTC leaf
7. The grade of the tea
   Ex: GFOP, BOP, BP

GRADES OF BLACK TEA

Because black teas comprise the largest share of worldwide tea production, the grading systems for both orthodox leaf manufacture and CTC black tea are the most elaborate. Yet they are easy for tea enthusiasts to determine. Africa, India, and Sri Lanka code their teas with a string of letters that correspond to these grades. For instance, you might see an Assam black tea being sold as Assam Khongea GFBOP or as Assam Kama Black FOP designation. Here is a breakdown of the designations you will see being used for both orthodox and CTC grades of Indian black tea.

GRADES OF ORTHODOX INDIAN BLACK TEA

Whole Leaf

SFTGFOP	Special, fine tippy golden flowery orange pekoe (smallest whole leaf)
FTGFOP	Fine tippy golden flowery orange pekoe (medium whole leaf)
TGFOP	Tippy golden flowery orange pekoe (medium whole leaf)
GFOP	Golden flowery orange pekoe (large whole leaf)
FOP	Flowery orange pekoe (extra-large whole leaf)
FP	Flowery pekoe
OP	Orange pekoe

Broken Leaf

GFBOP	Golden flowery broken orange pekoe
GBOP	Golden broken orange pekoe
FBOP	Flowery broken orange pekoe
BOP 1	Broken orange pekoe one
BOP	Broken orange pekoe
BPS	Broken pekoe souchong
OP	Orange pekoe

GRADES OF CTC TEA

Broken Leaf

FP	Flowery pekoe
PEK	Pekoe
BOP	Broken orange pekoe
BP1	Broken pekoe one
BP	Broken pekoe
BPS	Broken pekoe souchong

BLACK TEA

The Perfect Cup: Specifics for Steeping Black Tea

Many tea enthusiasts feel that black tea invites the addition of milk and sugar. For others, a spoonful of honey is all that is needed to balance its natural astringency. Black tea is best drunk however you like it—with a squeeze of lemon to accentuate astringency, or straight-up plain.

Indeed, a dash of milk or cream in a bracing cup of black tea is a comforting flavor combination that can make the gloomiest day seem bright. In the West, black tea often accompanies light foods at breakfast or lunch, and cakes and desserts in the afternoon. In many hotels of the world, afternoon tea is a grand affair that began long ago as a social occasion for "proper" ladies. "Taking tea" is a British reference to the habit of taking a pause from the business of the day to relax and enjoy a cup of fragrant, hot black tea.

The following measurements will work whether you are using a *gaiwan*, an individual teacup or mug, or a teapot, and can be scaled up directly. When you become familiar with a tea that is new to you, adjust to your taste.

MEASUREMENT	WATER TEMPERATURE
2 teaspoons for leafy tea; 1 teaspoon for orange pekoe grades or CTC (per 6 ounces of water)	190° to 200°F

STEEPING TIME	NUMBER OF STEEPINGS
3¹/₂ minutes for small leaf or CTC tea; 3¹/₂ to 5 minutes for orthodox leaf	One (possibility for a second steeping of large orthodox leaf, only if briefly steeped for the first infusion)

The Role of Black Tea

Black tea is the favorite choice of many tea drinkers worldwide. As complex and varied as wine, tea similarly can be either a life study or a simple, calming daily ritual.

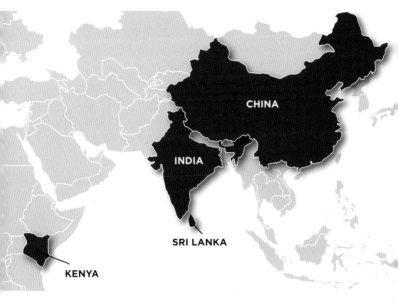

Major Tea-Producing Countries and Regions: Black Tea

BLACK TEA IN AFRICA

The tea industry is relatively new in Africa; it was only in 1903 that the first tea bushes were planted on a two-acre tract in Kenya. Despite this brief history, Kenya ranked third in world production of black tea in 2008.

Tea is grown in nearly every country in Africa, but much of it is not available in the United States. The largest tea producer in Africa is Kenya, and tea gardens flourish on both sides of the Great Rift Valley in elevation ranging from 4,900 feet to 8,850 feet. The majority of Kenya's tea is black tea—a tiny amount is manufactured into green tea.

Kenya teas have vigor in the cup and are flavorful and full-bodied in style. While a few tea producers concentrate on orthodox leaf, self-drinking teas, 95 percent of Kenya's leaf (as is true for most African countries) is manufactured into the less expensive CTC tea that goes to the United Kingdom, the United States, and other countries for use in strong, darkly colored proprietary tea blends.

After Kenya, Uganda, Malawi, Tanzania, and Zimbabwe produce the largest quantities of African teas.

BLACK TEA

BLACK TEA IN CHINA

China produces only a small quantity of black tea—less than 15 percent of their yearly production. But there are many exquisite black teas to be found from Anhui, Fujian, Guangdong, Henan, Sichuan, and Yunnan Provinces.

The quality of Chinese black tea is very high—the sweet, soft nature of leaf plucked from China bush varietals and cultivars provides an underlying delicious, nonastringent flavor that is enhanced by the distinct Chinese style of withering and oxidation.

As one would expect from the country that first figured out how to make black tea (all tea, in fact), the process of black tea manufacture in China is unique to Chinese tea producers. Chinese black teas are influenced by a longer wither (which underscores fragrance), a longer, slower oxidation (which tones down astringency in the liquor and concentrates flavor), and the desire to maintain the distinctive appearance of each tea's leaf.

China's tradition of this longer wither and slower oxidation of black tea (a trait carried over from other tea manufacture) is based on the best way to accentuate the "made" tea, which is directly related to the pluck. All classes of Chinese tea rely on a quantity of sweet-tasting buds to plump up the flavor of the tea: buds are richest in amino acids and polyphenols. This is why Chinese black teas are smoother, sweeter, juicier (less dry), and more buttery (less astringent) than black teas from other sources.

Chinese black teas do not have the very dark, undifferentiated appearance of many other black teas. Instead, depending on the variety or cultivar of tea bush, you will notice that the tea leaves will be gray-black or brown-black in color. Some tea, such as Imperial Sichuan and Keemun Congou, are comprised of small whole leaves or budsets, while other teas, such as high-grade black tea from Yunnan Province, are comprised of large, brown-black leaves and a quantity of juicy buds.

Especially delicious are Yunnan black teas, which are known as *dian hong*. These are made from buds and/or leaf plucked from older tea bushes (rather than from modern cultivars planted in new tea gardens). These teas are instantly recognizable because they are either bud-only or consist of lovely, long, and slightly twisted russet-brown leaves with an abundance of golden buds. The flavors of these teas are soft and caramel-sweet; they have very little astringency, but instead offer a substantial amount of enticingly warm and appealing aroma.

BLACK TEA IN INDIA

When many tea drinkers think of "tea," they think of Indian black tea. Commercial tea cultivation in India has a unique history that dates only to the mid-nineteenth century. Prior to that time, the leaves of indigenous tea trees in the northeast state of Assam were used by local tribes to produce a simple, caffeinated brew.

Today, India produces black tea in a diverse group of fifteen states. From the northern states that border the lofty Himalaya to the tropical river valley of the Brahmaputra River and the lush Nilgiri Mountains in the southern states of Kerala and Tamil Nadu, India produces a broad variety of tea in a full spectrum of styles, tastes, and prices. From 60 to 75 percent of the total tea production in India is Assam tea, 1 percent is Darjeeling, and 25 percent is Nilgiri tea; the balance is comprised of lesser-known teas from other regions of the country.

Assam

The Assam region is situated geographically in the northeastern corner of India, bordering on the countries of Bhutan to the northwest and Burma to the east. Assam is the birthplace of India's indigenous tea bush: *Camellia sinensis* var. *assamica*. This variety of tea bush produces larger leaves than *Camellia sinensis* var. *sinensis* (China bush) and thrives in this lush tropical region.

During the cropping season, Assam's tropical weather brings either seasonal rains and sweltering heat and high humidity, or periods of intense sunshine and high heat. Because of the tropical weather, tea production in Assam is virtually year-round work, paused only for the finicky monsoon season and any necessary pruning.

The majority of Assam's black tea is manufactured into CTC tea, contributing overall strength and backbone to black tea blends (primarily sold in tea bag form). In India, CTC tea is used in prodigious quantities to make India's celebrated spiced tea, chai. A small quantity of delicious, premium-grade, orthodox whole-leaf tea is made by some Assamese tea producers, but it is difficult for these producers to sell orthodox leaf at the price they need to receive for the extra work involved in manufacturing it because overseas buyers focus on Assam's less expensive CTC tea. Assam tea is produced from the combined efforts of an estimated 800 to 850 classified tea gardens (those over 500 acres in size), another 500 to 800 gardens awaiting classification, and approximately 200,000 to 300,000 small tea growers.

Darjeeling

Darjeeling is India's most celebrated tea and one of the world's most famous. In the nineteenth century, the reputation of Darjeeling tea became firmly established in England as a "fancy tea."

Darjeeling is a mountainous area located west of the Assam region in the northern state of West Bengal. It is truly a "Kingdom in the Sky," blessed with a lofty Himalayan environment and outstanding *terroir* that produces tea unlike any other on the planet. Here, variations in climate bring long cold winters, cool and breezy summer months, and late summer monsoon rains. This geography and climate provide a well-balanced set of growing conditions for superb high-mountain tea.

The Darjeeling area is comprised of eighty-seven tea gardens spread over seven valleys of what is collectively known as "the hill." Here, tea gardens thrive at elevations from 1,800 to 6,300 feet. As the elevation climbs, the cool, thin air slows leaf growth, yielding smaller tea leaves. This slower maturation concentrates the flavor in the leaves, giving these teas a well-defined, precise flavor profile.

Due to the high elevation and steep grade, tea gardens here are not as large as those planted at lower elevations. This results in smaller annual harvests of this exquisite tea. Accordingly, the price of fine Darjeeling tea is high, as worldwide demand has never waned for pure, unblended Darjeeling tea.

Darjeeling tea gardens are planted with both *Camellia sinensis* var. *sinensis* (China bush) and *Camellia sinensis* var. *assamica* (Assam bush). But it is the China bush variety that gives Darjeeling tea the distinctive "muscatel" flavor that has made this tea so popular.

Tea-garden owners sell their tea under their garden name or mark, such as Castleton Estate or Goomtee Estate. The best Darjeeling teas are sold by lot number (called an "invoice") that pegs each lot's manufacture to an exact day of a specific month, but rarely does the consumer see this detail.

Seasonal weather plays an important role in the outcome of any given batch of tea. The price of pure Darjeeling in any given year reflects demand plus the quantity and quality of the tea, depending on the weather conditions leading up to and during the time of plucking and manufacture.

Nilgiri

The states of Tamil Nadu and Kerala in southern India share a portion of the Nilgiri (Blue Hills) Mountains. Here the Western Gnat Mountains in Kerala meet the Nilgiri, creating a series of spectacular high ridges that reach as high as 8,202 feet in elevation. Tea bushes thrive in the perfect tea-growing weather here, and Nilgiri's beauty is completed by lush forests, tropical jungles, streams and rivers, and sunny high plateaus.

Nilgiri teas are plucked all year long, but they have two distinct seasons that account for 65 percent of the annual

BLACK TEA

Nilgiri yield. Springtime brings the first teas to market, but the best teas of the year are made from the winter-plucked teas. These are gathered from December through March, and their delicious flavor is a direct result of the beneficial effect that the cold air has on the slow development of flavor in the leaves.

Despite the southern locale of the Nilgiri Mountains, there is always the threat of frost in the high valleys during this season. It is not so cold that the plants go dormant, but frost always threatens. In these conditions, a light coating of daily frost slows plant growth, allowing the flavors in the leaf to concentrate. These teas are known as frost teas and they exhibit vibrant, fresh, intriguingly spicy aromatics. The Nilgiris are affected by two monsoon seasons each year, which bring the tea gardens alternating rainy and dry seasons.

Today a handful of large estates and more than 20,000 small landowners located in six districts (Panthalur, Gudalur, Udhagamandalam, Kothagiri, Coonor, and Kundah) are responsible for the production of Nilgiri tea. Most Nilgiri production is CTC tea, but a handful of producers are returning to fine-quality orthodox tea.

BLACK TEA IN SRI LANKA

Small in size but mighty in tea production, this tropical island paradise produces some of the world's finest black tea. Ceylon tea became world famous when Sir Thomas Lipton became the first tea seller to use "place of origin" as a designation of quality on which to build brand popularity and loyalty. Today, we have a renaissance of interest in *terroir* and all of the unique aspects of taste and flavor that place confers on food products.

Tea was first cultivated in Ceylon by the English in 1875. Prior to this, Ceylon was a coffee-growing island, but a succession of devastating coffee blights wiped the coffee plantations out of business. Bolstered by their successful experiment with tea cultivation in Assam, India, in the mid-nineteenth century, the British began to plant tea bushes on the island where coffee trees once grew. By the end of the nineteenth century, Ceylon farmers had a created a successful new venture with tea production.

Today, the island is known as Sri Lanka, but the tea is still sold as Ceylon tea. These teas are famous for their fine, elegant, flavorful orthodox style. Once marketed in England as "The Cup That Cheers," these teas have added flavor, color, and finesse to many fine English tea blends.

Sri Lanka benefits from a near-perfect location and geography, and it has an enviable microclimate that introduces a complex set of factors (temperature, moisture, and wind) that greatly benefits the personality and style of these teas.

Sri Lanka experiences two monsoon seasons, which give all of the tea regions a rainy as well as a dry season, and a season of best-quality tea. When the monsoon is drenching one part of the island, the other part is experiencing optimal weather conditions of cool, clear days and bright sunshine for prime tea production.

Tea grows in central Sri Lanka, in six well-known tea-growing districts, each of which features a different elevation: Dimbula, Kandy, Nuwara Eliya, Ruhuna, Uda Pussellawa, and Uva. The most important tea grows at the highest elevations, and in Sri Lanka that means roughly 4,000 to 6,500 feet high. As a group, the teas are brisk and full-bodied, not flowery or robust. The highland teas are thirst-quenching and self-drinking teas. They are prized for their fragrant aromas and clear, bright colors, which range from golden to coppery. Ceylon teas are not designated as first- or second-flush teas, but are labeled by region, district, estate, and grade.

A very small amount of CTC tea is made (less than 6 percent of production) as well as non-estate-specific black tea blends. All genuine Ceylon tea bears the logo of the Sri Lanka Tea Board as a mark of authenticity and pride.

Plucking Style for Black Tea

The plucking standard for black tea in most tea-producing countries is a hand-plucked bud and two leaves. This is the optimum plucking standard for fine-tea manufacture—in fact, it is called a "fine pluck," and most gardens follow this plucking standard with little deviation throughout the season. When a tea garden wishes to produce a small quantity of an exceptional, limited-edition tea, they might pluck an "imperial pluck"—the bud and one leaf—for this.

Because of their precious nature, small yield, and subsequent effect on the quantity of tea during the remainder of the plucking season, buds alone are rarely plucked for black tea manufacture (while often plucked for green tea and white tea). Of course, there are a few exceptions to this, most notably Yunnan Golden Buds and Assam Golden Tips.

In fact, China has several exceptions to the fine-plucking standard because different teas require a certain set of leaves to achieve the necessary appearance and taste. The most well-known plucking standards are *mao feng* (bud and two leaves) and *mao jian* (bud and one leaf) tea. Other teas require that the plucking standard be a bud and three to four leaves.

Some Chinese teas are known as *refined* teas, and these are sorted by size and graded into several categories. Other Chinese teas, such as Keemun Mao Feng, are known as *unrefined* teas. These are teas made for a short time once a year from a specific pluck and are not graded into several categories.

The method of leaf plucking varies in black tea–producing countries. For example, all leaf is plucked by hand in the tea gardens in China, India, Kenya, and Sri Lanka. In some countries, hand-plucking means removing the budset from the plant only by finger-plucking; in other places, small hand-held cutters or shears are acceptable plucking tools.

Motor-driven leaf cutters can be small and require only that two people working in tandem hold the machine steady over the row of tea bushes while slowly moving it over the tops of the bushes. Or these machines can be large industrial harvesters that are driven over the rows and tops of the tea bushes and clip with massive extended cutters. Either way, more than just leaf is removed, and the resulting flavor of these teas is inferior to tea made from leaf of the same size that is carefully and intentionally plucked by hand.

The Harvest Year: Seasonal Plucks for Black Tea

Depending on the country (or the region), the cropping season (seasonal plucking times) begins in spring or in winter, as in China and Taiwan, or the season may persist in a continuous cycle nearly year-round without a period of weather-induced dormancy, as in the tropical weather zones of Assam, Sri Lanka, Indonesia, southern India, and Africa.

In most tea gardens, tea bushes flush with the most vigor and finest new growth in the spring. It is this reawakening after a dormant period that produces the first plucking, which for many teas is the year's tastiest crop. As tea plants circulate the nutrients that have been stored in their roots over the winter throughout the plant, the bushes "flush" with new leaf and the leaf fills with plant juices. This continues throughout the months of the growing season as the bushes are plucked, but not all seasons produce leaf of the same quality.

There is a time in every tea season when the batches of leaf are superior. The tastiest tea comes as a result of particular weather phenomena during certain seasons. In general, summer growth is rapid and pluckers must contend with weeks of rain. As a result, the leaf swells with water and grows rapidly. If plucking is not done on a regular basis (as often as every seventeen days) the leaves become large and tough. As a result, the flavor of summer tea is often dull and lacking in focus.

In the fall, cool, shorter days slow plant growth, and moisture in the leaf is reduced. Leaves can once again be plucked when they are small and tender in size. Fall tea often rivals spring tea for flavor and aroma.

In regions where plants do not go dormant in winter, growth slows, allowing the plants to gather and concentrate plant juices in the leaves. Spring brings "awakening," not as dramatic as dormant bush bud-break; however, late winter and early spring signal the first major harvestable flush of newly revitalized buds and leaves of the year. Late-winter pluck and spring leaf are generally considered the best from these regions.

BLACK TEA PLUCKING STYLE IN CHINA

China's bushes that produce leaf destined to become black tea have a dormant period in the winter. Depending on the location and elevation of the gardens, some tea bushes awaken from dormancy in February, others not until the end of March. While there are fewer Chinese early spring black teas than green tea brought to market, Bai Lin Gong Fu and Yunnan Dian Hong Golden Buds are two examples of stupendous early-plucked bud black tea.

Spring is the primary cropping season for all classes of premium Chinese tea, although production of commercial-grade tea continues into summer. The autumn harvest picks up again for some black teas.

- Spring: Golden Buds, fancy keemuns, Panyangs, Imperial Sichuan
- Summer: High-altitude mountain harvests, field-grade China blacks
- Autumn: Panyangs, Yunnan Fancy
- Winter: Hibernation

BLACK TEA PLUCKING STYLE IN INDIA

Tea cultivation in India began in northern India in the low-lying jungle regions of Assam before spreading to West Bengal and the high Himalaya Darjeeling region. Over time, significant tea gardens were established in the southern regions of Tamil Nadu. Extremes in geography and weather conspire to create distinctly different teas that closely identify with the *terroir* of their respective places.

Assam

The tropical rains and heat that characterize this watershed region of the Brahmaputra River bring forth an abundance of tea that crops nearly year-round. The best teas come from the summer season, before the monsoon rains arrive.

- Early spring: First-flush tea
- Late spring/early summer: Summer tea
- Midsummer/early fall: Monsoon teas
- Autumn: Autumnals
- Winter: Some harvest in the north, little in the south

Darjeeling

At this high elevation, tea bushes have a winter dormant period. Tea is harvested during:

- Early spring: First flush
- Late spring/early summer: Second flush
- Summer/monsoon flush: This is less distinctive, coarse leaf that is used primarily in commercial tea blends
- Autumn: Autumnals
- Winter: Hibernation

Nilgiri

Tea is plucked year-round, but two cropping seasons provide the best-quality seasonal tea:

- Frost tea: Winter flush (December to March)
- Spring tea (April and May)

BLACK TEA PLUCKING STYLE IN SRI LANKA

The tropical weather in Sri Lanka allows for leaf plucking all year-round. But the best leaf comes from particular months of the year when nearly perfect weather brings the finest, most distinctive teas—known as "quality season" teas—to market.

- Central Highlands (Kandy and Nuwara Eliya): Year-round production. Quality season: February
- Eastern Districts (Uda and Uva): June through October production. Quality season: July
- Western Districts (Dimbula): December through April. Quality season: February
- Southern District: Ruhuna (Morawak Korale): Quality season: February and July

BLACK TEA

Leaf Manufacture: Production Methods for Black Tea

In countries where tea cultivation was begun by the British (Africa, India, Sri Lanka) or the Dutch (Indonesia), black tea is made by one of two manufacturing processes: orthodox or CTC (cut-tear-curl).

Orthodox black teas are whole leaf (and broken leaf) that are gently processed into well-twisted leaves that are separated into clearly marked grades with specific standards of leaf size and grade. Orthodox leaf implies hand-plucked, premium tea. Orthodox tea represents only 5 to 10 percent of the black tea produced each year. The steps of orthodox tea manufacture are roughly the same for all black tea: withering, rolling, roll-breaking, sifting, oxidation, drying, and grading.

CTC tea is made by a process involving cutting, tearing, curling. CTC tea is made from leaf that has been ripped and shredded, then rolled into pieces that have a choppy, granular appearance. CTC teas may be hand-plucked or sheared with hand tools or machine-harvested, but the process results in commercial tea whose flavor is masked by the strength of the liquor. CTC tea now accounts for roughly 90 percent of all black tea produced today.

Orthodox teas are more costly than CTC because orthodox tea manufacture requires more skilled workers and many additional steps to accomplish the task. At one time, all tea was made completely by hand. In the late nineteenth century the British devised mechanical processes and the machinery to replicate in the tea factory the steps that had been done by hand in village workshops. Today, this machinery is the mainstay of much tea production. In the 1930s, the CTC process was introduced.

CTC was initially devised as a way to process damaged or low-quality leaf that was otherwise unusable. But CTC eventually turned into a new, convenient way to process tea for tea bags and for black tea blends where the concern was for the strength of the liquor and immediate release of color into the cup rather than finesse of flavor and distinctive expressions of *terroir*.

Black teas steep the strongest liquor in the cup (with some exceptions made for Chinese Pu-erh tea). The color in the cup ranges from coppery red to dark orange-black. Orthodox leaf is appealingly clear and bright in appearance. A pleasant astringency or "pull" in the mouth is expected in a well-made orthodox black tea, and flavors are often described as "bright" or "brisk."

Look for black tea at the extreme end of an oxidation chart. It is classified as 100 percent oxidized leaf, which is sometimes mistakenly reported to be fermented. It is the complete oxidation of the leaf that is responsible for the distinctive, characteristic flavors and aromatics of black tea.

Black tea manufacture is more complicated than green tea manufacture but less complicated than oolong production. All black tea producers utilize a series of steps that guides the fresh leaf through the process, but tea makers in different locations make adjustments in these steps to accommodate their climate and weather conditions, the size and condition of their fresh leaf, and so on. After the fresh leaf is brought to the tea factory, black tea manufacture involves withering, rolling, roll-breaking, sifting, oxidation, and drying.

During manufacture, it is the series of chemical reactions brought on by the controlled manufacture of the polyphenols in the leaf that results in the unique appearance, taste, and aroma of black tea. Specifically, the natural internal leaf juices (or cell sap) contained within the tea leaves is "released" from the cells during the rolling process. The next step, roll-breaking, allows the internal leaf enzymes and polyphenols to mix and spread evenly throughout the leaf, and sets the stage for the polyphenols to absorb oxygen during the early stages of the oxidation process. This transformation of the polyphenols is what gives black tea its texture and astringency, characteristics that define this class of tea. As with all classes of tea, the polyphenols also provide the healthful benefits of tea.

BLACK TEA

PU-ERH TEA

Perhaps the most exotic tea in China's vast repetoire of astonishing tea is Pu-erh. China is the only country that makes Pu-erh tea, and everything about Pu-erh tea is enticing, including the place where it is made: Yunnan Province in southwest China. Here, the Pu-erh tea–producing area lies in the southwest quadrant of the province and encompasses many counties in and around the tropical Xishuangbanna region.

It is safe to say that if one is looking for a lifelong obsession in the world of tea, then look no further than Pu-erh. Pu-erh offers tea enthusiasts many tastes: new Pu-erh, vintage Pu-erh, sheng Pu-erh (natural post-processing fermentation), or shou Pu-erh (artificial fermentation).

The first thing that draws visiting tea enthusiasts to Pu-erh in the tea shops in Yunnan Province is the fantastic appearance of the tea. The display in a well-stocked Pu-erh tea shop is a real head-turner. It is not unusual to see *tongs* (bamboo-wrapped stacks of individually compressed disks or cakes of Pu-erh tea) of Pu-erh overflowing the shelves, with one tea cake from each *tong* on display so that customers can see the colorful wrapper and assess the information printed on it. These enticing wrappers are printed in Chinese, but feature the name of the tea factory along with other essential pieces of information.

Over time, Pu-erh has been compressed during manufacture into a dizzying array of other intriguing shapes and sizes as well: squares, rectangles, oversized mushrooms, little coins, and domes (with a pushed-in hollow core) that range from one-ounce sizes that resemble a hummingbird's nest to melon shapes (symbolizing bounty and prosperity) that can weigh as much as sixty pounds. Some Pu-erh is made by pressing the leaf into a hollow bamboo tube and drying it over a fire.

But despite all of these attractive shapes, Pu-erh is most commonly shaped and sold as a compressed, flat disk. These

tea cakes are thin and round (about eight inches in diameter) and are called a *beeng cha*. Loose-leaf Pu-erh is also made in several grades from the same leaf.

Pu-erh is China's famous fermented tea. Yes, fermented it is, and gloriously so. At the root of traditionally made Pu-erh is a host of bacteria, molds, and fungi (*Penicillium chrysogenum, Rhizopus chinensis, Apergillus clavatus,* to name a few) that thrive in the moist, tropical weather of Xishuangbanna and live in the air and on the fresh tea leaf throughout the forests, villages, and tea factories in Xishuangbanna. Were it not for these simple organisms and the transformative magic that they bring to young Pu-erh cakes, vintage Pu-erh cakes—and Pu-erh in general—would not exist. Pu-erh has finally been "discovered" by Westerners. This is ironic since Yunnan

Province is considered to be (along with parts of neighboring Assam, India; Burma; Laos; Thailand; and Vietnam) the ancient birthplace of tea. Pu-erh developed from tea-making customs deeply rooted in the history of the people living in and around the tea forests located in the mountains of this region. The tradition of allowing tea bushes to grow wild and to develop into tall forest trees began here thousands of years ago because that is how nature established the first forest tea groves and how early people found them. Long before the rest of China knew of tea, people inhabiting this area made a great discovery: the leaves of a certain kind of tree gave them strength and vigor when chewed and eaten.

Soon after, the leaves of these indigenous tea trees were used to make a simple tea concoction. While this drink bore no resemblance to tea as we know it today, it did provide a basis for the tea trading that has existed between Yunnan, Sichuan, and Tibet and other people along China's northern border for thousands of years. Today, local tea trading is very

Classic Leaf Styles (Shapes) of Manufactured Pu-erh Tea (Dry Leaf)

Loose-leaf:
- Twist
- Needle or wiry
- Leafy chunk

Compressed or packed:
- Bricked or caked
- Bowl or cup

Pu-erh Tea Flavor (Taste) Components

Pu-erh varies incredibly because of the existence of both loose-leaf and compressed styles, and its great variation in age. Pu-erh's flavor components are among the most exotic in the world of tea and are well worth exploring.

- Aromatic
- Biscuity
- Body—full
- Brisk
- Character
- Colory/coppery
- Earthy
- Full
- Heavy
- Herbaceous
- Lingering finish
- Musty
- Smooth
- Soft
- Strength
- Sweet
- Woody

active among people living in Yunnan and along the borders of Burma, Laos, and Vietnam.

During the Han dynasty, (206 BC–220 AD) dried leaf from Yunnan tea trees was sent to the cities in eastern China. Leftover broken bits of tea and discarded leaves were compressed into tea cakes and transported to northern border populations of Mongols, Tartars, and Tibetans, who found the hot drink a beneficial addition to their meager diets. The compressed cakes became an ideal way to load large quantities of tea onto the backs of horses and mules for the long trip over the mountain route to Lhasa, the capital of Tibet.

Under the Tang dynasty (618–907) a vast network of tea gardens were cultivated in southern and western China to increase tea production. As greater quantities of tea began to be sent to Tibet, the Chinese devised a trade exchange of tea for strong, healthy Tibetan horses. The horses were essential for the Chinese army to use in fending off enemy groups from the north, while increasing the tea trade with Tibet opened up a new market for China's tea.

These trade routes, collectively known as the Tea Horse Road, thread their way across a series of rugged mountains from Yunnan to Tibet. Later, several additional routes from tea-production zones in Sichuan were added, until six routes (with hundreds of local side paths) were created.

By the time of the Song dynasty (960–1179) historians estimate that close to two thousand traders and mules plied these routes with cargo each day, and that it took as long as six months for the journey to reach completion. More than seven thousand tons of tea, along with salt, sugar, cloth, and other essential goods, were carried over the Tea Horse Road each year.

Despite the perilous travel over some of the most inhospitable terrain on earth, this road was consistently used until the mid-1960s. At that time, a paved road was constructed, allowing modern transport vehicles to convey tea from Yunnan up into Tibet. Today, the ancient road still connects remote villages one to another, but the caravans of goods, animals, and men have ceased. However, Pu-erh tea continues to be made.

PU-ERH TEA

Gallery of Pu-erh Teas

SHENG PU-ERH
(raw, uncooked, or green Pu-erh)

REGION: Yunnan Province, China

STYLE: Open leaf and buds, compressed into a round cake

MANUFACTURE: Not oxidized prior to natural postproduction fermentation

FLAVOR: Smooth, sweet, and lingering, deep woodsy flavor (umami)

AROMA: Lightly herbaceous, with the clean fragrance of vigorous plant material plucked in a healthy forest, and well-made *mao cha* (primary tea unique to Pu-erh)

LIQUOR: Clear burnt umber, tinged with a golden amber hue

STEEPING: Numerous short infusions at 205° to 210°F. Drink plain.

Sheng Pu-erh has incredible depth of character, with a flavor that has been likened to the essence of the forest floor. It is said that Pu-erh broth (the term Pu-erh connoisseurs use for the tea liquor) tastes deliciously "of the good, clean earth." Developed from years of experimentation going back to the days of the Tea Horse Road, Pu-erh is one of the unique examples of *terroir* that exist to help us celebrate centuries-old tradition. Sheng Pu-erh is rarely sold as loose-leaf tea, and the cakes are wrapped individually and marked with information detailing the village or tea factory that manufactured it.

SHOU PU-ERH
(ripe, cooked, or black Pu-erh)

REGION: Yunnan Province, China

STYLE: Open leaf and buds, plus some broken leaf

MANUFACTURE: Oxidized prior to artificial fermentation

FLAVOR: Smooth, deep, more pronounced "fermented" taste

AROMA: Bold, earthy, and reminiscent of damp leaves, mushrooms, or a forest floor after a rain shower

LIQUOR: Deep burnt-umber, tinged with a red-orange hue

STEEPING: Numerous short infusions at 205° to 210°F. Drink plain.

Shou Pu-erh is virtually ready to drink as soon as it is purchased and does not offer the challenges of aging that sheng Pu-erh does. It is less of an acquired taste and more of an everyman's Pu-erh in China. Shou Pu-erh has a lingering, funky, dank flavor and aroma reminiscent of tree bark and rich, moist soil. Shou Pu-erh is more accommodating in taste than its sheng counterpart when both are drunk young.

Shou Pu-erh is a modern variation of traditional sheng Pu-erh; the base leaf in cooked Pu-erh is oxidized and undergoes artificial, accelerated fermentation before being compressed. Shou Pu-erh is made into tea cakes and is also commonly found in loose-leaf form. It is more reasonably priced than sheng Pu-erh.

PU-ERH TEA

Tips for Purchasing
Pu-erh Tea

Learning about Pu-erh and detecting the differences between sheng and shou Pu-erh is a fun hobby that involves lots of tasting, study, and sleuthing for information. *Beeng cha* are individually wrapped, in tissue-thin paper, thick paper, or cloth wrappings. Tea producers wrap stacks of seven tea cakes with bamboo bark (naturally shed from large bamboo trees) and secure the bundle with bamboo thread, string, or wire to make a *tong*, which is how Pu-erh tea cakes are stored and sold by the tea producers to tea shops and to avid Pu-erh collectors.

RECIPE FOR A *BEENG CHA:*
FROM *MAO CHA* TO PU-ERH

Each year Pu-erh tea producers create numerous Pu-erh cakes. Like carefully blended grapes in the creation of some fine wines, each tea cake can be a blend of leaf grown in various locations in Yunnan. Or it can be comprised of leaf from a single place. Some *beeng cha* recipes are made from wild arbor tea tree leaves plucked exclusively on one of the famous tea mountains, another tea cake might be a blend of wild and semi-wild leaf from two places, or a tea cake may be made from buds only.

Before being made into tea, the leaf used for making Pu-erh is processed in a very simple manner. Once dried, the leaf is called *mao cha*. Unlike the majority of other Chinese teas, Pu-erh is made from *mao cha* and not directly from freshly plucked leaf.

GRADES OF PU-ERH TEA

The lower the number, the smaller (and younger) the leaf. While grade alone does not indicate quality, the size of the raw materials used can point savvy tea enthusiasts to the type of leaf they prefer.

Grade	Leaves
1 and 2	Early spring buds and shoots
3 and 4	Mid-spring buds with a low percentage of small leaves
5 and 6	Average-size leaves
7 and 8	Large, older leaves
9 and 10	Largest, oldest leaves

Grades one through four are grades often used to make fancy compressed shapes and highest-quality loose-leaf Pu-erh. Grades five through nine are used for *beeng cha*, bricks, and high-quality loose-leaf Pu-erh. The largest leaf from the oldest arbor trees is not given a grade, but cakes that are made with these leaves are noted as such.

PU-ERH LABELS

There are more than a dozen large tea factories in Yunnan (and many smaller ones) producing many different brands of both sheng and shou Pu-erh. To identify the producer or brand, a small printed paper *nei piao* (description ticket) is placed on top of the cake under the wrapper. Additionally, a smaller, square piece of paper is embedded in the tea leaves just under the surface of the *beeng cha*. This is called a *nei fei* (inner trademark ticket), and is a stamp of authenticity for the cake. Large-sized batch tickets called *dia piao* are attached to bamboo baskets that contain multiple *tongs* of Pu-erh.

Pu-erh tea factories print batch tickets with a coded number that identifies when the tea cake recipe was started, the grade of the leaf used, the code that identifies the tea factory, and a three-digit batch number.

For example, the number "8853" refers to a recipe that began in 1988, that was made from grades #5 and 6 leaf, and that was produced by factory #3, the Xia Guan Tea Factory.

Since a *beeng cha* can be purchased to drink now or be put away for aging, how old the tea cake is when it is purchased determines how much of a head-start on aging it has, and of course, the cost of the *beeng cha*. The following will give you an idea of the structure of Pu-erh *beeng cha* from least to most expensive:

- New Pu-erh (1997–present)
- Seven-Son Era Pu-erh (1972–late 1990s)
- Masterpiece Era Pu-erh (1950–1972)
- Antique Pu-erh (earlier than 1949)

Accordingly, for those without a working knowledge of the Chinese language, and, equally important, an in-depth understanding of how to interpret the information given on a Pu-erh label, this information can seem overwhelming. Indeed, the possibilities are many and varied; and unfortunately, counterfeit Pu-erh is being made in other regions of China. It is best to begin learning about Pu-erh by putting your faith in a trusted tea merchant who can guide you through the maze of details regarding Pu-erh.

When purchasing Pu-erh, decide whether the cake is for aging or to be drunk now. The best for aging are sheng Pu-erh cakes, as they are the result of *mao cha* that has been allowed to undergo natural, spontaneous post-processing fermentation after the tea cakes are made. While they can be drunk now, they will taste better after they age.

Shou Pu-erh or ripe *beeng cha* are made from *mao cha* that has undergone an artificial fermentation process in the tea factory. These tea cakes have the ability to mellow over the course of a few years without deteriorating, but they do not age.

While volumes have been and continue to be written in Asia about Pu-erh tea, the opportunity to find good-quality sheng Pu-erh in the United States is limited. Historically this tea has been virtually nonexistent here and little known to Western tea drinkers. This is slowly changing as interest in Pu-erh blossoms. It is difficult to recommend specific *beeng cha* to look for in the States because the odds of finding specific tea cakes here is small. Instead we are providing a listing of names of Pu-erh tea factories to look for when searching for Pu-erh. Most of these producers are large factory producers who primarily use plantation tea (*tai di cha*, or leaf used to make Yunnan green and standard Yunnan black teas) rather than leaf from old trees. We suggest that you start your foray into Pu-erh with tea from these producers, and then, if you decide that Pu-erh is for you, branch out into small production tea cakes from tea villages that use old tea tree leaf.

Recommended Pu-erh Tea Factories

* Changtai Tea Factory
* Chun Guang Ming Yuan Factory
* Dadugang Tea Factory
* Fengqing Tea Factory
* Kunming Tea Factory
* Liming Tea Factory
* Lincang Tea Factory
* Menghai Nanqiao Tea Factory
* Menghai Tea Factory
* Ming Yuan Chung Guang Factory
* Shuan Jiang Meng Ku Factory
* Tienyuan Tea Co., Ltd.
* Xiaguan Tea Factory
* Xishuangbanna Jingmai Tea Co., Ltd
* Yunnan Dali Najian Tea Co.
* Yunnan Simao Ancient Pu-erh Industry Co., Ltd.
* Yunnan Xishuangbanna Mengyang & Guoyan Tea Factory

The Perfect Cup: Specifics for Steeping Pu-erh Tea

Gaiwans and small unglazed clay teapots are the preferred vessels for steeping Pu-erh tea. In fact, they are the only vessels that tea connoisseurs in Asia use to steep this tea.

Pu-erh tea can be successfully re-infused many times. In fact, it should be steeped this way in order to enjoy the many phases of flavor that these short infusions will deliver. Pu-erh will not be your "rushing-off-to-work-in-the-morning" quick cup of tea, but it might become your evening or weekend pursuit when drinking tea with a gathering of tea-loving friends.

Pu-erh, with all of its variables of age, leaf material, and sheng or shou production styles, is not as straightforward as

PU-ERH TEA

other teas for giving precise leaf-to-water ratios and steeping time guidelines.

Here are a few pointers to get you going; the rest of your Pu-erh tea steeping education will come with experimentation. Keep notes on the tea you steep, the optimum water temperature, the number of re-infusions, and re-infusion times, and you will find your personal assessment of the results becomes a valuable reference tool.

1. Choose a *gaiwan* or an unglazed clay teapot that is between 150 and 200 ml (roughly 5 ounces to 6 3/4 ounces) in size.

2. Fill the vessel one-quarter full with Pu-erh that you have broken off from a *beeng cha* and separated into leaves and small pieces. If you are weighing your tea, use approximately 4 to 5 grams per 100 ml of capacity. Ideally, a 150-ml pot or *gaiwan* will require approximately 3 tablespoons (5 to 6 grams) of tea; a 200-ml vessel will need approximately 4 tablespoons (6 to 7 grams) of tea, but you can add more or less leaf as your taste for and experience with Pu-erh expands.

3. Pu-erh needs the hottest water of any tea. Use water that is just off the boil, at 205° to 210°F.

4. The first pour of water is the "rinse water" for washing the leaves. Pour it on and immediately pour it off.

5. Add more hot water and steep the tea for twenty-five seconds. Drain the tea into a tea pitcher and serve. Let the tea cool for a few seconds before drinking it to better appreciate the flavor.

Here are some infusion time recommendations to get you started. When you feel like experimenting, increase steeping times by increments of ten and fifteen seconds until the flavor begins to diminish. Loose-leaf shou Pu-erh can be steeped like black tea, whether you are using a *gaiwan*, an individual tea cup or mug, or a teapot, and can be scaled up directly, whereas a good sheng Pu-erh might not scale directly.

INFUSION TIMES	
Infusion Number	**Time**
First	Rinse (rinse a second time if the tea is an old *beeng cha* or if it seems particularly dusty)
Second	25 seconds
Third	30 seconds
Fourth	35 seconds
Fifth	40 seconds
Sixth	45 seconds
Seventh	50 seconds
Eighth	55 seconds
Ninth	60 seconds
Tenth	90 seconds

Major Tea-Producing Countries and Regions: Pu-erh Tea

The Role of Pu-erh Tea

The usual legend told about how Pu-erh tea came to be is that during the months-long journey that Pu-erh traveled the distance of the Tea Horse Road (beginning in the Tang dynasty, 618–907) to Tibet, the tea underwent many changes in altitude and passed through pockets of weather that ranged from blazing hot sunshine to forbidding snowstorms. By the time the tea reached its destination, it had fundamentally changed. The leaves had acquired a darker color, and the tea had "ripened." The flavor of the broth (the term for Pu-erh tea liquor) was richer, earthier, and mellower. The tea had benefited from enzymatic changes caused by natural microbial fermentation of live organisms present within the leaves in these crudely made tea cakes. Eventually, Pu-erh tea became highly sought after by all classes of people.

This story suggests that aged tea (tea that is transformed into something wonderful by the slow progress of time) was not known before the long journey that tea made along the Tea Horse Road. But, it is entirely possible that the benefits and value of aging tea was known before that. Old Daoist mendicant monks (and shamans before them) would have been in a position to observe the ability of tea to age well under the right conditions. So too would the tribal people living in the forests of Yunnan and along the border with Burma and Laos (where indigenous tea trees were also located), who packed tea into bamboo tubes and buried them for keeping and ripening.

So, whether or not the ripening of the tea after its departure from Yunnan was expected by the tea men who made the tea, or how much the changing environments that the tea passed through added influence to the taste of the final product, is most likely a question still awaiting an answer. It is possible that the information coming back to the tea makers helped them better understand the dynamic potential of their tea. With luck, a student of tea or a tea historian will find a trace of information that sheds light on this chicken-or-the-egg question.

From that time forward, Pu-erh tea makers produced *beeng cha* for domestic consumption within China, and began utilizing conditions in the tea factories that would maintain sufficient moisture in the tea leaves during production. Tea cakes were also stored in humid conditions for periods of time so that the microbial activity continued to work its magic on the tea without a journey on the Tea Horse Road.

Today, this ancient tea still enjoys a steady popularity in China and is finding new tea enthusiasts in the West. In the late twentieth century, a new style of shou Pu-erh was created for everyday tea drinking. These two types of Pu-erh now compete for market share in China and abroad.

Pu-erh tea and Yunnan's tea-drinking culture is unique in China. As with other distinctive Chinese teas, it all begins with unique tea plants. The best Pu-erh is made from large leaf *mao cha* that has been plucked from old tea trees. Lesser quality Pu-erh is made from fresh leaf plucked from cultivated tea plantation bushes (*tai di cha*).

In the tea mountains of the Xishuangbanna and Simao regions of Yunnan, ancient tea trees can be several hundred years old (or older!) and grow more than twenty feet tall amid the lush forest environment. These broad-leaf arbor species of indigenous *Camellia sinensis* are a far cry from their tame and cultivated tea bush cousins that blanket the hillsides in tea gardens around the world. The leaf from these trees is known as *Yunnan dayeh*, and the large buds and leaves can grow to be nearly the size of a human hand.

The best Pu-erh is made from arbor-style buds and fresh leaf that are collected from tea farmers and villages in more than thirty counties. It is the quality and substance of this raw material coupled with traditional processing techniques and the sultry tropical temperature of this region that combine to make Pu-erh tea so unique and delicious.

In the best cases, the forests and old tea trees create a rich biodiversity and natural environment that yields the sound raw leaf without the use of fertilizers or pesticides. These ancient, old-growth tea trees have been tended for centuries by local populations of ethnic people inhabiting the region

PU-ERH TEA

(the Bai, Dai, Hani, Jinuo, Lahu, Yi, and Wa), who share a long history with these tea mountains. The forests of old tea trees are a living inheritance for these people, who own much of the land and are caretakers of these forests. The tea trees provide a livelihood for the local people and by protecting the health of the tea trees and forest this generation will ensure the future of their children. Invigorated Pu-erh interest from the West will help ensure that these old tea trees and forests continue to receive the care and respect they deserve.

SHENG PU-ERH (NATURAL POST-FERMENTATION)

This is the favorite of tea enthusiasts and Pu-erh collectors. The sublime nature of sheng Pu-erh is a combination of factors that reflects the *terroir*, careful manufacturing techniques, proper storing, and benefit of slow aging over a period of years.

When the tea farmer and the tea-factory workers have done their part to make the tea cake a success, it is time for the microbial activity to begin its magic. It is the presence of live organisms on the surface of the tea leaves (and spread throughout the tea cake) combined with humidity and the passage of time that results in the mellowing of a once astringent young leaf, transforming it into something rich and mouth-filling.

Some say that the taste of Pu-erh is suggestive of beef broth, mushrooms, and the earthiness of the forest floor, and that these qualities also give Pu-erh umami, the sixth taste often found in fermented or aged foods. In a well-made *beeng cha*, these are desireable qualities. Even a young *beeng cha* that is made from ancient tea tree leaves and carefully crafted can have good taste and good *cha-qi* and show promise for something even better in the future. The positive energy of *cha-qi* brings contented feelings of bliss and relaxation to those who drink the tea. Pu-erh has some of the strongest *cha-qi* of any tea, especially vintage sheng Pu-erh cakes that have had years to gather their strength.

Sheng Pu-erh is also appreciated in tea circles for the range of tastes, aromas, and sensations that develop in the mouth and throat of the tea drinker, and for the length of the flavor, or *hui gan,* on the palate. In Chinese tea parlance, *hui gan* refers to flavor that returns sweetly and resonates in the mouth and on the breath. Sheng Pu-erh can be drunk young, but at this stage many tea cakes can be bitter and unbalanced because the best flavor is still to come after a decade or so of careful aging.

Sheng Pu-erh is said to have five distinct characteristics:
- High-mountain arbor tea tree leaves
- A profusion of spring buds and large leaf
- Taste that is sweet and distinctive
- Refinement of age
- Strong *cha-qi* (positive energy from a good environment)

SHOU PU-ERH
(*WO DUI* ARTIFICIAL FERMENTATION)

During the mid-twentieth century, the idea of bringing a "quicker-to-age, faster-to-drink" version of Pu-erh to market began to take hold. Modern-style Pu-erh was developed in a government tea factory in the 1970s in response to this demand using *wo dui*, or wet-pile fermentation, as a method of artificially accelerated fermentation.

In the early days of shou Pu-erh manufacture, the tea was not as fermented as it is today. Formerly, the tea cakes could ripen to a degree on their own. Today's shou Pu-erh will mellow if stored properly and will keep for several years, but it is not capable of natural post-fermentation changes. Shou Pu-erh has a strong fermented taste and is drunk in many households in Hong Kong and eastern China. In Hong Kong, dim sum restaurants serve shou Pu-erh tea, where it is known as *bolei.*

Plucking Style for Pu-erh Tea

The fresh leaf is gathered in the forests and brought to the village tea factory, where it is fixed only to a certain point and then dried to a stable state. At this stage it is called *mao cha*, and to make it, the leaf is de-enzymed to remove excess moisture, then rolled and twisted to stimulate enzyme action, and finally air-dried or sun-dried to stabilize the leaf. *Mao cha* is drunk by people in the tea villages, but *mao cha* is not Pu-erh; it must undergo further manufacture to become Pu-erh.

The Harvest Year: Seasonal Plucks for Pu-erh Tea

Old tea trees are plucked from April to July. Small tea-producing villages are dispersed throughout the tea mountains, and many tea growers sell their *mao cha* to private tea factories for processing. Much of the *mao cha* is used by village tea factories to make their Pu-erh cakes, but large quantities are also sold to the large, privately owned tea factories that were at one time government controlled.

Place-specific Pu-erh cakes are very desirable. For instance, *beeng cha* can be made from *mao cha* gathered from just onc mountain, such as Youle, Gedeng, or Yibang, or pressed from *mao cha* that was gathered from several mountains, such as Menghai, Jinggu, or Bulang, and blended together.

Pu-erh factories make scores of *beeng cha* every year, and many tea enthusiasts are loyal to their favorite recipes and factories. Some Pu-erh recipes become very popular and are repeated every year; other recipes may not be so successful. Creating a new Pu-erh recipe introduces a multitude of possibility, and requires the knowledge of a veteran tea maker who knows the taste of each *mao cha* and what each will bring to the mix. *Mao cha* determines the flavor of the tea cake, and how the different leaf is combined affects the surface appearance of the tea cake. It is common practice for the tea workers to put better, larger, and prettier leaf on the outside of the cake and work the smaller, less attractive leaf into the inside of the cake.

Leaf Manufacture: Production Methods for Pu-erh Tea

Both sheng and shou Pu-erh are made from *mao cha*, but the methods of leaf manufacture differ in significant ways. In essence, the leaf in sheng Pu-erh is not oxidized, but it is oxidized when making shou Pu-erh. In either case, the first step is to blend the *mao cha* in the tea factory (if the tea cake is to be made from blended leaf). If the leaf is unblended, then this step is unnecessary.

SHENG PU-ERH PRODUCTION METHODS

Tea cakes are made in village tea factories as well as large tea factories. The steps used in both productions are essentially the same, although several methods vary in approach. Village tea cakes reflect the history of traditional Pu-erh production, as they are still made close to the way that *beeng cha* was made in the past.

Artisan Village Production

Village production usually means that the *mao cha* has been made from fresh leaf collected from old tea trees in the local forest area and sun-dried in the traditional manner. Work is carried out in a simple tea facility and relies on traditional techniques, such as using heavy stone weights to shape and compress the tea cakes. These weights do not compact the tea with as much force as the hydraulic presses used in large tea factories do, so these tea cakes "breathe" air more readily. This allows the microbial activity within the tea cake to work its magic on the tea faster and better. The leaves stay more intact when the cakes are pressed by stone, and it is easier to break off chunks of tea for steeping because the cake is less dense.

PU-ERH TEA

Factory Production

We had the opportunity to visit the Xiaguan Tea Factory, which is famous for their *tuo-cha* (nest-shaped) Pu-erh, the very tea we observed in production. The *mao cha* is blended by the workers before they pack it into the perforated mold that will shape the *tuo-cha*. Two workers sat with two bags of *mao cha* in front of them, and they put some leaf from each bag into the mold in such a way that the smaller leaves were tucked inside the *tuo-cha* and the larger, more attractive leaves were visible on the surface.

The difference between the factory and the village production begins with the quality of the *mao cha*, the speed and carefulness of the process, and the degree of compression the cakes receive. In the Xiaguan factory, production is truly assembly-line production work, at a pace so fast that it was difficult for us to really grasp what the workers were doing. Essentially, after the mold was filled with the right quantity of *mao cha*, the mold was passed to another worker, who placed the mold in a cloth pouch and then set it over a steam source and dampened the *mao cha* with moist, hot steam. The pouch was passed off to another worker, who flipped the pouch over and removed the metal mold. The pouch was passed to yet another worker, who gathered the *mao cha* in the bottom of the pouch and placed it under the hydraulic press. In less than forty-five seconds, the *mao cha* was formed into the desired *tuo-cha* shape. Cloth bags seemed to fly through the air as the *tuo-cha* were quickly removed and placed on movable racks and taken to the drying room. Rapidly, cloth bags were gathered up and returned to the previous work station for refilling.

Some tea factories make stone-pressed Pu-erh as well, but one imagines that the production of this, too, is sped up and not quite executed in the spirit of the old traditional way. This factory-made Pu-erh, while considered good, does not have the benefit of the slower methodology used in village tea production or the fresh air conditions found in village tea factories.

Happily for Pu-erh tea drinkers, there is a Pu-erh made for every taste and budget in China. For those who favor sheng Pu-erh, these tea cakes are identifiable by the presence of large, complete tea leaves that thread their way throughout the tea cake. The leaves are usually a blend of colors: mottled green-gray to light brown–dark chestnut brown to whitish, and the surface of the cake is slightly uneven and feels loosely compressed. The cakes have a clean, appealing, natural aroma. The knot indent on the back is usually slightly offset and a bit irregular in shape.

SHOU PU-ERH PRODUCTION METHODS

Shou Pu-erh is made in tea factories using the *wo dui* process. *Wo dui* begins by spreading the *mao cha* in a deep pile on the factory floor, and the leaf is dampened with mists of water. After the proper dampening, a thermal blanket is put over the pile of leaf. Heat builds up in the pile, encouraging both oxidation of the leaf and fermentation as enzymatic changes start to occur within the leaf. This heat buildup encourages the viability of the natural bacteria present on the leaf, stimulating and initiating the fermentation process. The pile is turned every day or so to allow each leaf to spend some time in different layers of the pile. When we visited the Menghai Tea Factory, we were told that their *wo dui* process takes sixty to seventy days to complete. After *wo dui* is completed, the leaf is dried to a moisture level of approximately 10 percent.

After this stage, the leaf is compressed and shaped in a hydraulic machine. The tea cakes are then put in a drying room, where they will rest and continue to dry on racks before being wrapped.

Leaf that has undergone *wo dui* turns dark, and it sometimes resembles fully oxidized black tea. Red-orange or brown tips can be present, but the leaf on the surface of the cake is short and uniform in size. The tea cakes have a strong aroma of the forest floor, and they feel heavy and solid from hydraulic compression. The knot indent is very uniform and regular.

PU-ERH TEA

Scented Tea

During China's Ming dynasty (1368–1644), the art of scenting tea with the heady aroma of fresh flower blossoms presented the leisure class with a delightful new taste experience. Sweet flower fragrances have always been adored in China, so it would have been viewed as quite an accomplishment when clever tea men perfected the art of scenting various green, white, or black teas with the very essence of jasmine, magnolia, osmanthus, or rose blossoms.

Today, the art of scenting tea continues, especially in the vicinity of the town of Changle, in Fujian Province. Fine-tuned skills are necessary to create these lovely teas, as well as the patience necessary to allow the natural scenting process to occur slowly and correctly. The most popular scented tea is jasmine tea, and in this procedure, fresh jasmine flower blossoms are comingled with semiprocessed tea leaves (called *zao pei*) numerous times over the course of several days or weeks. The result is superbly scented tea: each batch of tea can require as much as ten pounds of fresh flowers for every one pound of *zao pei*. In fact, the highest grades of jasmine tea can be scented as many as nine different times and can take nearly one month to be properly scented.

JASMINE DRAGON PEARLS

REGION: Fujian, China (and other provinces)

MANUFACTURE: Fresh jasmine flower–scented tea

STYLE: Budsets scented before, during, and after being rolled into pearls

FLAVOR: Smooth, sweet, and soft; traditionally scented

AROMA: Clean, sweet, and floral

LIQUOR: Clear silver

STEEPING: Two or three 2- to 3-minute infusions at 165° to 180°F (the scenting will dissipate slightly after the first infusion). Drink plain.

Jasmine Dragon Pearls has been popular for several centuries. With the essence of the jasmine flowers captured within the tightly rolled tea buds, the minimal surface area of the pearls guarantees that they are able to hold their scent well. Fun to watch unfurl and delicious to drink, Jasmine Dragon Pearls captivates the tea enthusiast as the aroma wafts up from the cup. Easy to measure, Jasmine Dragon Pearls can usually be counted instead of measured or weighed. Using eight to ten pearls for every six-ounce cup of water will produce tea house–ready results.

JASMINE SNOWFLAKES

REGION: Sichuan Province, China (and a few other provinces)

MANUFACTURE: Fresh jasmine flower–scented tea

STYLE: Budset and leaf, scented during manufacture (then freshly dried flowers are added to the finished tea)

FLAVOR: Smooth, sweet, and focused; highly scented, with a lingering finish

AROMA: Bright, sweet, and very floral

LIQUOR: Clear silver

STEEPING: Two or three 2- to 3-minute infusions at 160° to 170°F (most scenting dissipates after the first infusion). Drink plain; in Sichuan Province this style of tea is often chosen to accompany the local spicy-hot cuisine.

Highly scented jasmine tea differs quite significantly from traditional-style jasmine tea. The scenting of the leaf is much higher, requiring that more flowers be added to the base leaf. Flowers are also added to the finished tea, a visual appearance appreciated in Sichuan Province and parts of northern China, near Beijing. Jasmine tea can vary wildly in price, with the modern versions usually at the costlier end of the spectrum due to the increase in labor and materials. Specialized tea masters supervise the manufacture of highly scented jasmine tea due to the complexity of the timing and the number of variables needing to be coordinated.

Measuring Tea: Volume to Weight

The volume to weight difference of tea leaf is important to understand as you experiment with steeping tea from different classes or several different leaf styles within the same class. (See pages 35–36 for more information on steeping instructions.)

Each portion of tea in these photographs weighs two grams. Because every tea has its own unique leaf shape, leaf size, and density, we measured each two-gram portion to see what the quantity of each tea would be. This is what we found:

- Green tea: Longjing—2 teaspoons
- White tea: Bai Hao Yin Zhen—1½ tablespooons
- Oolong tea: Tieguanyin ("Monkey-Picked")—1½ teaspoons
- Black tea, orthodox manufacture: Keemun Mao Feng—2½ teaspoons
- Black tea, CTC manufacture: Tanzania—1 generous teaspoon

The old standard of "a teaspoon per cup" applies only fine-cut black tea. Today's premium, artisan whole-leaf teas (which represent all the classes of tea manufacture) require that tea enthusiasts use different amounts of leaf per six-ounce portion of water to produce a flavorful cup with the proper soluble solids in the liquid tea.

So, start with a recommended amount of leaf and water, and adjust to your taste as you become familiar with a particular tea or style of tea.

Longjing

Tanzania

Bai Hao
Yin Zhen

Keemun
Mao Feng

Tieguanyin

CHAPTER FOUR

TEA STORAGE AND FRESHNESS

Tea, like freshly roasted coffee and aromatic spices, possesses delicate aromatics that will deteriorate when exposed to the flavor-robbing influences of air, heat, and humidity. For the best protection, store tea in a clean glass or tin container to preserve its flavor and soundness. Depending on the type of tea, most properly stored tea will keep for a minimum of one year; the same tea stored carelessly may lose its goodness in just two or three months. Of course, some oolong, black, and Pu-erh teas store well for longer than one year, but for the majority of green, yellow, and white teas, it is best to replenish with fresh tea once the seasonal harvest brings new tea to market.

Air is the enemy of tea. Left unwrapped, air will rob tea of its vibrant flavor as well as the residual moisture content of the leaf (and yes, even though tea is a "dry" product, all tea has about 5 percent residual natural moisture remaining in the leaves). When this happens, tea becomes brittle and takes longer to rehydrate, resulting in a cup of tea that tastes flat, dull, and out of balance.

In tea markets around the world, tea is often sold from uncovered baskets, boxes, or large bags. Tea sells very rapidly in these markets, so freshness and condition are not a problem, especially in tea-producing countries. Conversely, tea shops around the world that specialize in premium tea keep their tea protected in glass jars, tins, and metal boxes with tight-fitting lids, and ensure that the tea stock is properly rotated (first in, first sold).

Storing tea in glass is fine as long as this method is suitable for the environment of the shop. When you are in a tea shop that sells tea from glass jars it is essential to know whether the store has a busy tea counter. Providing that there is a constant turnover of tea and the jars are not sitting under bright lights or in direct sunlight, this is a wonderful way to be able to see the leaf before purchasing.

Storing Tea at Home

Most retail tea merchants sell their tea in tin tie bags or zippered foil or paper pouches. These bags are fine for short-term storage, but our advice is to repackage all loose-leaf tea (anything larger than a sample size that does not come packed in a tin). Many tea shops sell decorative glass jars, tea tins, and ceramic containers made of porcelain, unglazed clay, or stoneware for storing tea at home.

PROTECTING TEA FROM LIGHT AND HEAT

Constant exposure to strong light will fade tea leaf, and the tea will lose flavor. Keep tea away from heat-generating places such as sunny windows, radiators, the top of your refrigerator, countertops that are close to under-cabinet lighting in the kitchen, the kitchen stove, and even the computer station at work.

When purchasing tea that is weighed to order for you, look to see where the light sources are. If the tea is stored near a bright sunny window, the tea could be receiving several hours of direct sunlight during the day, exposing it to unnecessary heat and color fading. Strong but diffuse overhead room lighting is fine as long as accent lights are not shining directly on the tea.

PROTECTING TEA FROM ODORS

Tea readily absorbs odors, so store tea away from spices or other aromatic foodstuffs (such as garlic) in your pantry. Avoid new or recycled plastic containers for tea storage; plastics often have persistent, hard-to-eliminate odors, particularly if they have previously contained other food.

TEMPERATURE CONDITIONS FOR STORING TEA

It is better to keep tea at an even temperature than in fluxuating temperatures. Tea stores better in cool temperatures over hot temperatures and in humid conditions over bone-dry air.

The question of keeping tea in the refrigerator (or the freezer) comes up regularly—this is a thorny question. In China, Japan, and Taiwan, many green and oolong teas are vacuum-packed in five- or ten-kilo packs after manufacture and kept in very high-tech temperature-controlled refrigerators at temperatures that are close to freezing. The "vacuum-packed" aspect of this storage method is crucial to its success. Both refrigeration and freezing are beneficial for many foods, but they can be harmful to tea. Freezers are drying by nature, and refrigeration introduces moisture and refrigerator "smell," both enemies of tea. Our advice is to store tea in air-tight containers at ambient temperature and never put tea in the refrigerator or freezer.

Freshness and Shelf Life of Tea

As is true for some wine, a number of teas, such as highly oxidized oolongs, sheng Pu-erh, and some black tea, can and will, under the right set of conditions, keep well and age into something magnificent.

To enjoy your tea at its optimum, you must determine when the tea was harvested. In all tea-producing countries leaf is plucked and finished tea is manufactured according to a seasonal timetable. This seasonal cycle is repeated at approximately the same time every year (give or take allowances for major weather situations such as droughts, torrential rains, earthquakes, and so on), just as we expect the return of lilacs in spring or the first local tomatoes to reach the farmstand in summer. For premium Chinese, Japanese, and Korean green teas, spring is the only season during which these teas are harvested.

For instance, Japanese Gyokuro tea is only made once a year beginning in the middle of May and ending by the middle of June. New-crop Gyokuro becomes available in any current year once production concludes. Therefore, Gyokuro sold in a tea shop in Japan or America in January or February of any given year is from a prior year's harvest. When in doubt, inquire about the pluck date of the tea that you are considering purchasing. This is the only way to know how old it is. A good tea vendor will know this information and be proud to let you know that their tea is fresh. It is important, though, to understand what your tea vendor might mean when, for example, it is stated that they will have a new batch of a certain tea in their shop in two weeks. This may not mean that it will be new-crop tea; it may only mean that what is expected is another shipment of more of the same tea that they already had.

So it pays to become familiar with the seasonal harvest dates of tea (by class of tea) so that you know how to interpret the information you are given. For example, if you adore the first-flush Darjeeling that was just air-flown in to your local tea shop from India in the early spring, from the current year, you should feel free to purchase as much of it as you wish because no more of it will be made until the spring of the next year.

Don't always assume that the "one year for best freshness rule" always applies. A reputable tea vendor will stop selling any tea that has faded in flavor and replace it with something better tasting or fresher. Some teas hold better than others—much depends on the quality of the fresh leaf at the time of manufacture, the integrity of the leaf manufacture, and the storage conditions before and after purchase. In a great year when the weather leading up to harvest and the weather during harvest cooperates, that crop of tea can be as long-lasting as it is spectacular in flavor. Tea from such a harvest may hold well for a year or two past the "expected" freshness date. Because the age of some tea is so closely tied to freshness, it is important that the age of the tea and the quantity of it that you purchase be in sync. While premium tea does not have a "best before" date, you may not want to stock up on a pound of your favorite green tea if the new-harvest green teas will be arriving at your tea vendor's shop in a few weeks' time. So it pays to ask when the tea was plucked and when the next harvest of that tea will be before purchasing a significant quantity.

When you purchase new tea, be mindful of the all-too-common trap of misguided frugality, which is drinking up the old tea before starting to drink the new, or saving your good tea for "special occasions." Don't let perfectly fresh and lovely tea sit around while you finish up tea that you have on hand. There is no value in tea that may be past its prime. Except for a few types of tea that can be aged successfully, remember this golden rule: for the best flavor, greatest amount of antioxidant benefit, and sheer pleasurable enjoyment, drink fresh tea from the current year's harvest.

Each of the six classes of tea has its own parameters of freshness, keeping ability, potential for aging, and amount of time after manufacture that the tea will have optimum flavor, as do the separate categories of new tea and aged tea. With black, oolong, and Pu-erh tea, the more highly oxidized the leaf, the longer the flavor lasts, and the better its keeping ability will be.

STORING GREEN, YELLOW, AND WHITE TEA

Green teas are not made with longevity in mind, and there is little one can do to enhance long-term keeping qualities. In fact, some green teas begin to lose flavor around six months past harvest and manufacture. But small-leaf green teas have less surface area and are often tightly curled, which keeps their surface area to a minimum and their freshness intact, sometimes well beyond the one-year standard. Tightly compacted green, yellow, and white bud-only teas are dense and have a longer keeping ability than do their large, leafy counterparts. Because they have less exposed surface area than leafy teas do, they can retain flavor for one full year or longer.

STORING OOLONG TEA

The style of oolong manufacture and the corresponding amount of oxidation and roasting affects the keeping ability of oolong tea. Highly oxidized strip-style and traditional-style roasted semiball-rolled oolongs can age deliciously for decades. As they mature, it is customary to refresh or re-roast these oolongs once a year to eliminate moisture and "awaken" the flavor. Modern-style unroasted semiball-rolled oolongs and open leafy–style oolongs can keep for one to three years, depending on the tea. Wu Yi Shan rock oolongs last longer than Feng Huang Dan Cong teas, which last longer than roasted Tieguanyin (from Fujian and Taiwan) and Tung Ting teas, which last longer than unroasted High Mountain gao shan, Baozhong, and Bai Hao oolongs.

STORING BLACK TEA

The more intact the leaf, the better the tea will keep. The more finely cut the tea, the more surfaces there are for the air to come into contact with it and rob the flavor. In general, black teas can be kept for one to three years. Whole-leaf, orthodox-manufacture black teas last longer than CTC teas, which last longer than broken-leaf, orthodox-manufacture teas.

STORING PU-ERH TEA

Pu-erh tea cakes store best in the same temperature conditions that we prefer to live in: 68° to 86°F, and they do better in humidity (70 percent or more) than dryness. (Humidity keeps the process of natural fermentation alive within sheng Pu-erh tea cakes.) Try to keep the cakes exposed to an even temperature and humidity throughout the year rather than exposing them to seasonal fluxuations in heat or air-conditioning. Do not refrigerate or freeze. Do not store *beeng cha* in plastic bags or wrap. Keep it in the original paper wrapping or wrap it in brown paper if the original wrapper is lost or torn.

Sheng Pu-erh will age gracefully and can be kept for twenty years or more under the right storage conditions. Shou Pu-erh undergoes accelerated aging and does not *improve* with the passage of time, but it will *keep* well for a decade or more in good storage conditions. Loose-leaf Pu-erh mellows with age and keeps well for two to three years, or sometimes longer in good storage conditions.

Aging Tea at Home

In Asia, one can easily purchase aged oolong and Pu-erh teas. But here in the States, aged teas are not readily available, and the oldest and rarest aged teas are simply not for sale here. So aging your own tea is the *only* way to ensure that you will have an impressive stash of delicious, mature tea down the road. The only requirement is purchasing the right kind of tea and storing it carefully.

Sheng Pu-erh cakes are made with aging in mind. Purchase the best-quality young cakes you can and stash them away for a decade or two (or longer). The older they become, the better they will taste, and the more valuable they will be. Because tea cakes contain so much tea, you can take the cakes that you are aging out of storage every now and then and steep a pot to enjoy the transformation of the leaf as it ages.

If one is willing to gamble a little, it is possible to age other types of tea as well. Remember, there is a big difference between "stale" tea and "aged" tea. Not all tea will age, and some will age beautifully. Start by aging a darkly oxidized Wu Yi Shan rock oolong or Feng Huang Dan Cong. Take a quantity of tea—say, a quarter pound or a little more (so that you can steep a bit here and there and taste its development)—and put it into a ceramic or clay jar that is a good fit for the quantity of tea. Close the jar and leave it in an even-temperature environment for one year.

Then open the jar and smell the tea—it should smell good, and much like it did when you put it in there, or a little better. Steep a few leaves and leave the rest in the jar. Let it continue to age several more years and then take a little bit out and brew it in your "for dark oolongs only" Yixing teapot. By now, the flavor will be maturing to something impressive and distinctive.

Patience pays off. The more years you let the tea sit, the better it will be. The aged teas that we have tasted displayed the expected flavor characteristic of the tea in the cup, but their richness and depth of flavor filled it with more life and energy than when the tea was young.

GLOSSARY

Aroma. (steeped tea liquor) The scent released from the leaf as a result of steeping; a suggestion or preview of the combination of the brisk flavor components and the taste attributes inherent in the leaf. There are two of types of aroma: the fresh, clean, or dull aspects that show style and quality of manufacture, and the floral, nutty, or grassy descriptors that the palate will amplify.

Astringency. (steeped tea liquor) A sensation of drying felt throughout the mouth, similar to what mixologists refer to as "pull" (an essential quality in a great cocktail), this sensation is refreshing and satisfying, thirst-quenching, and stimulating all at the same time.

Baked or bakey. (steeped tea liquor) An overly fired leaf, not a positive toasty or smoky characteristic; a negative dry, over-cooked taste.

Basket-fired. (fresh leaf) An artisanal process traditionally used in green and yellow tea manufacture in which fresh leaf is fired to prevent oxidation and finish-fired using the same equipment—a locally woven basket of varying diameters and heights (depending on the leaf) placed on and off over embers for as long as necessary to shape and dry the leaf. A similar basket-firing is also used sometimes as a part of traditional white, oolong, black, or Pu-erh firing.

Beeng cha. (finished tea) The unit of measure for traditional compressed Pu-erh. *Beeng* translates to "biscuit" or "cake" in reference to the shape of the disk. Approximately 375 grams, they can be made in half-sized or oversized disks as well.

Biscuity. (steeped tea liquor) An aromatic term used most frequently with black tea made from Assam bush, this is a positive attribute that indicates proper manufacture and the presence of the signature malty taste that Assam bush teas should possess.

Bloom. (finished tea) A leaf luster indicative of careful sorting and handling.

Body. (steeped tea liquor) The sensation of viscosity on the palate, variously subcategorized as light, medium, or heavy, in reference to the concentration of heft as sensed by the sides of the tongue; also known as *fullness*; the opposite of the term *thin*.

Bolt, bolted, bolting. (steeped tea liquor) The phenomenon, common to modern Darjeelings and several astringent green teas, wherein the brisk flavor components suddenly overwhelm the body characteristics and the cup qualities become unpleasantly assertive and harsh.

Bright. (steeped tea liquor) Indicates a clean, clear style that refreshes the palate; the opposite term is *muddy*.

Brisk. (steeped tea liquor) Having an appropriate amount of astringency; a palate-stimulating infusion that is not heavy and will readily accept the addition of dairy (if desired). Brisk teas are of necessity well made. The opposite term is *soft*.

Bud-only pluck. (fresh leaf) Bird's beak, lark's tongue, and sparrow's tongue are several of the pictorial transliterations from the Chinese used to describe an early-spring bud-only pluck from certain varieties of *Camellia sinensis* var. *sinensis* that sprout small tender buds. The reference is obvious— these tiny buds strikingly resemble the shapes of these ornithological features.

Budset. (fresh leaf) The pluck of an emerging bud and one or two leaves. This term encompasses both *mao feng* and *mao jian*—see page 186.

Clean. (finished tea) Tea that is free of debris, odd-sized particles, excess dust, and so on.

Clean. (steeped tea liquor) Indicates purity of flavor and an absence of any off-tastes; the opposite term is *harsh*.

Colory or coppery. (steeped tea liquor) Specific to black tea, most commonly with orthodox leaf, a positive indicator of good pigmentation and general high-quality manufacture.

"Column of air" drying method. (fresh leaf) A hot air–firing and drying method in which dry hot air is fan-forced through piping into a vertical cylinder into which a perforated platform has been fashioned. On this screen, fresh leaf is squeezed and rolled by the handful; this handwork ultimately yields a slightly twisted, semi-rolled green tea.

Cream, creamy, or creaming. (steeped tea liquor) Refers to the amino acid precipitate that forms when steeped hot tea cools. Some teas cream more readily than others; creaming is an important factor in the marketing of liquid RTD (Ready-to-Drink) tea beverages.

Crepey. (finished tea) The crumpled appearance of a well-made, large, broken-leaf tea.

CTC manufacture. (finished tea) "Cut-tear-curl," a modern tea manufacture, in which the leaf is chopped to an even size during the process of being oxidized into black tea. The resulting finished tea appears evenly granular or pelleted. Used in reference to black tea, the traditional, primary style of manufacture is orthodox.

Cultivar. A unique member of a species that has been created by human intervention to fulfill a specific trait or need. Cultivars may be designed to be disease resistant, a particular color or shape, or to be more prolific, etc., and are expected to be stable in their characteristics.

Dan cong. (finished tea) The familiar term used by tea enthusiasts to describe the market grade of the highly oxidized oolong tea produced from the Feng Huang Dan Cong single-trunk trees in Guangdong Province, China. The higher grades of Feng Huang Dan Cong teas are always referred to by their full name, including the specific type of tea tree (known as its "fragrance").

Earthy. (finished tea or steeped tea liquor) A positive attribute in several premium varieties of green, oolong, and Pu-erh teas; however, the term can also negatively indicate improper storage.

Even. (finished tea) Used interchangeably with *make* and *neat*, these terms refer to tea that is consistent in size and correct to grade; indicates a well-made tea.

Fannings. (finished tea) The tea that remains after all the other market grades of tea have been sieved. Most commonly used in reference to black tea, this formerly derogatory term has found some fashion recently with those looking for inexpensive, strong tea to make into concentrate, chai, or tea latte beverages. See *muddy.*

Firing. (fresh leaf) The general term used to describe the heating and/or drying of the fresh leaf during the manufacture of green tea. *Firing* can also refer to an application of heat during the manufacture of any of the classes of tea.

Fresh. (finished tea) Indicates a new-crop tea or proper storage of any tea; not a positive component of an aged tea.

Frost tea. (finished tea) Specific to tea from the Nilgiri Hills (the Blue Mountains) in southern India, this tea is harvested during the coldest months of winter; however, due to the unique climate in these hills, buds do emerge at that time and the result is a tea similar to but different than white tea.

Fruity or stone fruit. (steeped tea liquor) A negative term in reference to black tea, as it indicates improper oxidation or firing; *stone fruit* is the customary positive descriptor for the aromatic quality of standard Formosa oolongs, as a familiar and engagingly enticing attribute.

Full. (steeped tea liquor) References a positive sensation of body and good heft; indicates a well-made tea.

Gaiwan. A ceramic vessel used either to steep a single portion of tea or as a small pot for oolong or Pu-erh tea service. It consists of three pieces: the tea-steeping bowl, a saucer, and a lid. Once practiced, one drinks or pours from a *gaiwan* using only one hand.

Granular. (finished tea) Properly made CTC tea. Used for standard tea bags, chai, concentrates, and caffeine extraction for the pharmaceutical trade; a few well-made granular teas can be quite delicious.

Green. (steeped tea liquor) In reference to most black tea this is usually a poorly made tea, hurried in the early processing so it tastes raw or underdeveloped; in green tea vernacular, *green* indicates a steamed leaf in the Japanese style and is good for the style.

"Green" or "German style" Darjeeling firing. (finished tea) A recent convention in which a Darjeeling is fired to leave a significant proportion of slightly oxidized leaf. This yields a cup that is astringent and thin, but reminiscent of an "old-style," first-flush Darjeeling and is very popular in Europe.

Harsh. (steeped tea liquor) Generally negative, indicates hurried manufacture or poor-quality leaf; also sometimes used as the description for tea that has bolted during steeping; the opposite term is *clean*.

Heavy. (steeped tea liquor) The most extreme heft of body.

High Mountain gao shan. (finished tea) Taiwan's most prestigious oolong teas are hand-processed, semiball-rolled modern-style oolongs. These teas grow in gardens over six thousand feet in elevation in Taiwan's central mountains.

Hot air–fired. (fresh leaf) The general reference for tea (of several classes) that has been fired and/or dried using moving hot air. These techniques include basket-firing, column-of-air drying, fluid-bed drying, tumble-drying, and others.

Huang ya. (finished tea) The Chinese term for yellow tea. Can be either a bud-only pluck or a budset, but *huang ya* is always plucked in early spring and consists of only the tender young growth of *Camellia sinensis* var. *sinensis*.

Koicha. (finished tea) One of the two classic matcha preparations, *koicha* is "thick tea," served during *Chanoyu*, the Japanese tea ceremony. Traditionally, *koicha* is served communally, with participants sharing the tea from one *chawan* (tea bowl). See *usucha*.

Light. (steeped tea liquor) The most minimal heft of body.

Make. (finished tea) See *even*.

Manufacture. (finished tea) The term used for the general description of everything that happens from the time the fresh tea leaf arrives at the factory (large or artisan) until it leaves as partially finished or finished tea.

Mao cha. (fresh or dry leaf) *Mao cha* is semi-finished, sun-withered leaf that has undergone traditional pan-firing, and is the base for sheng and shou Pu-erh.

Mao feng. (finished tea) Traditional premium green tea pluck: two leaves and a bud.

Mao jian. (finished tea) Traditional premium green tea pluck: one leaf and a bud.

Matcha. (finished tea) The finely powdered tea used for thick and thin beverage making. Premium matcha is made from tencha, a special grade of Japanese green tea in which the stem and veins have been removed from the leaf; this eliminates all extra chaff and fiber from the powder, yielding an incredibly smooth and rich tea that is used for *Chanoyu*.

Men huan or **"sealing yellow."** (fresh leaf) The term in yellow tea manufacture that describes the process used to encourage the leaf to reabsorb some of its own aromatics. Also known as "smothering," this step is unique to yellow tea manufacture and involves gently steaming and covering fresh leaf with a cloth. Yields a tea that is smooth and has no astringency.

Muddy. (steeped tea liquor) Showing an excess of particulate in the infusion; a generally negative opacity that tends to dullness; may also refer to the cult-brewing-style "tea latte" in which CTC tea is brewed "hard" with steam in an espresso machine.

Musty. (finished tea) This is an off-taste that indicates improper drying and potential mildewing.

Neat. (finished tea) See *even.*

Nose. (finished tea) Aroma (smell) of the dry leaf usually only indicates blatant or negative characteristics: smokiness; off-taste (tiredness); the intentional addition of a fragrance (as in flavored or scented teas); or contamination by a foreign odor. Unlike the aromatics of steeped tea, which can afford a glimpse of the ultimate flavor profile of the prepared tea, smelling the dry leaf reveals very little of an informative nature.

Orthodox manufacture. (finished tea) Traditional whole-leaf tea manufacture. Various grading systems are used in different countries to distinguish the finish-fired, sieved leaf particles, which range from very large whole leaves to tiny bits of broken leaf. Used in reference to black tea, the second, modern style of manufacture is CTC.

Oven-fired (baked or roasted). (fresh leaf) An efficient drying and finish-firing combination often used in tea manufacture. Can be used as the principal oxidation-preventing and drying method in the manufacture of green tea (such as for Japanese greens—*roasted*, or Chinese budget greens—*baked*) or as a post-oxidation finish-firing in the manufacture of black tea.

Oxidation. (fresh leaf) Simply, the term used for the chemical change due to a material's absorption of or reaction with oxygen, ex: a banana's browning or metal's rusting. In tea manufacture, *oxidation* refers to the process in which withered fresh leaf is encouraged to absorb a controlled amount of oxygen, facilitating the transformation of this withered leaf into oolong or black tea.

Pan-fired. (fresh leaf) The general reference for tea (of several classes) that has been fired and/or dried using a woklike pan heated over a wood, a charcoal, a gas, or an electric source. Used when the leaf is flat or bud-only, and a toasty or nutty flavor is desired.

Plain. (steeped tea liquor) An infusion that is simple and clear but lacks character.

Pluck. (fresh leaf) Can refer to the action of or the result of removing the bud-only, budset, or bud and as many as five or six leaves from a tea bush.

Pointy or point. (steeped tea liquor) The extreme of bright, a sharpness and piquancy that may be off-putting; an old-fashioned term used primarily in reference to black tea.

Ragged. (finished tea) Uneven sorting or poor manufacture; the opposite of the term *even*, this is never a good attribute.

Raw. (finished tea or steeped tea liquor) Similar to bitter and harsh; generally unpleasant; however, *raw* is also used to describe the most classic method of producing the compressed forms of sheng Pu-erh, such as *beeng cha* (in this case *raw* is used interchangeably with *green*).

"Rested" tea. (dry leaf) 1. When a finished tea is deemed too assertively astringent (green) to be drunk immediately upon finishing (primarily some green, oolong, and black teas), or 2. if it is determined that a tea should be smoother (primarily green and yellow teas) it can be set aside for a period of time (determined by an experienced tea maker) to mellow. Similar to aging but for a much shorter time.

Smoky or tarry. (dry leaf) When intentional (as with Lapsang Souchong), this term refers to leaf that has been traditionally smoked over charcoal or green wood; when the leaf has not been deliberately smoked, a *smoky* taste is generally the result of a flaw in manufacture (with a few provincial exceptions).

Smothering. (fresh leaf) See *men huan*.

Soft. (steeped tea liquor) Smooth, lush, and subsequently often (but not necessarily) timid in flavor; not a negative term; the opposite term is *brisk*.

Stone fruit. (steeped tea liquor) See *fruity*.

Strength. (steeped tea liquor) The totality of all the positive attributes of tea in the cup; the sum of the parts.

Subvariety. A naturally-occurring or wild derivation of a species with unique characteristics that distinguishes it from the other plants within its botanic species. Its designation will be the species name followed with var.xxx, both in italics. Ex: *Camellia sinensis* var. *sinensis.*

Tana. The covering used in Japanese tea gardens to reduce or eliminate the amount of sunshine available to the bushes during the final period of growth before harvest. Can be made from either bundled natural straw or reed or woven plastic mesh.

Tarry. (dry leaf) Old-fashioned reference to the intentionally smoked tea (Lapsang Souchong) when smoked heavily to produce a penetratingly smoky flavor. See *smoky.*

Tea liquor. (steeped tea liquor) The drinkable liquid produced when manufactured, fully finished tea leaves have been steeped in water for the appropriate amount of time. Term is used by both professional tea tasters and tea enthusiasts.

Tencha. (finished tea) The Japanese green tea from which premium matcha is ground. During its manufacture tencha is neither rolled nor folded to make it easier to remove all stem and vein fiber, which yields a finer, more evenly textured matcha powder.

Ten Famous Teas. Teas formerly held in reserve for the Chinese emperors, these teas today represent the premium growths and productions in their style.

Terroir. The combined influence of geography, weather, season of the pluck, tea bush variety or cultivar, and method of leaf manufacture that is responsible for the unique flavor of an individual tea.

Thin. (steeped tea liquor) A generally negative term that indicates an overly light brew that lacks the expected character of a proper cup of tea; can also be tea that has been steeped incorrectly or intentionally diluted; more negative than the term mild.

Tip, tippy, tippiness. (finished tea) Consisting of, or inclusion of, the budset; when appropriate, this is positive and an indication of a fine pluck; but not all teas should be comprised of or have tip, so tippiness may indicate the inappropriate addition of purchased tips.

Tong. A wrapped bundle of Pu-erh *beeng cha.* Usually containing seven beeng, the *tong's* wrapping is traditionally made from cut bamboo leaf, but cloth may also be used.

Tribute tea. Tribute teas include the Ten Famous Teas (see page 189) and those that in more modern times have also been found to be in high regard among Chinese tea scholars and experts.

Tumble-drying. (fresh leaf) One of the hot air–drying methods, this refers to placing almost-finished leaf in a large perforated drum rotary tumbler very similar to a dryer used for clothes laundry. Heated air is forced through the drum and vented. A very controllable and evenly drying finish-firing method used by many tea makers.

Tumble-firing. (fresh leaf) Refers to a part of tea manufacture during which the leaf is placed in a tumbler that looks very much like a cement mixer or candy panning machine. The leaf tumbled within this sharply angled cylinder obtains a balled or pelleted shape. Gunpowder green tea and the semiball-rolled oolongs employ this technique as part of their manufacture.

Umami. The Asian representation for the hard-to-describe sixth sense of taste that is often associated with mushrooms, soy sauce, and other earthy, texturally rich foods.

Usucha. (finished tea) One of the two classic matcha preparations, *usucha* is "thin tea," served during *Chanoyu,* the Japanese tea ceremony. Traditionally, *usucha* is served to guests in an individual *chawan* (tea bowl). See *koicha.*

Yan cha. (finished tea) The Chinese term for the top echelon of premium, plant-specific, strip-style rock oolongs from the Wu Yi Shan in Fujian Province. *Yan cha* are sought after by expert tea preparers and skilled enthusiasts, and are a good example of the stunning nature of unique teas from a specific *terroir.*

BUYER'S GUIDE

Thanks to the efforts of many tea vendors who are passionate about tea, awareness of pure, premium tea is growing and moving "beyond the tea bag" to a point of common knowledge. Our listing is intentionally short, and a bit contrarian. Rather than simply list a multitude of sources, we have chosen to compile a list of tea specialists of varying sizes and orientation who specialize in pure, premium whole-leaf tea and whom we feel are particularly passionate about their tea. To us, passion is not just about selling product, but also about educating one's customers about tea, sharing tea knowledge freely, and being diligent about the turnover (i.e., freshness) and provenance (origin) of their teas. Of course we wish all tea enthusiasts could experience the tea that we drink: offerings in the marketplace do differ considerably, and knowing where to look for premium tea is important. Our list represents those whom we believe stand out in the crowd for a job well done.

Assam Tea Company (online only)

www.assamteacompany.com

Saunam and Namgay Bhattacharjee operate their business from Vancouver, British Columbia. Their teas come directly from their family tea farms in Assam, India. Besides selling delicious, seasonal teas, Saunam is extremely knowledgable about Indian teas and the state of affairs regarding Indian tea farms and farmers. If you want to know what it was like to grow up on an Assam tea farm (and have a pet elephant), Saunam is the man to ask.

Camellia Sinensis

351 rue Émery, Montreal, Quebec, Canada

(514) 286-4002

www.camellia-sinensis.com

This shop and corresponding tea salon is the collaboration of four young men who each bring a different tea expertise to their business. They offer tastings, workshops, and a wonderful selection of hand-selected teas from around the world, and their dedication to tea is apparent by their extensive, informational website.

Den's Teas (online only)

www.densteas.com

Den Shirakata is a third-generation tea man who travels between his home here and his tea-production facility in Shizuoka, Japan. Den imports a wonderful selection of tea from his company—Shirakata Denshiro Shoten—which is a real treat for Japanese tea enthusiasts looking for authentic Japanese green teas from the most current harvest.

Hou de Asian Art (online only)

www.houdeasianart.com

Guang Lee and his wife, Irene, specialize in Taiwan oolongs and Pu-erh from Yunnan Province. They also have a nice selection of well-made, artisan Yixing teapots about which Guang is very knowledgeable. Hou de Asian Art is one of the only sources in the United States from which tea enthusiasts are able to purchase copies of the lavish tea magazine *The Art of Tea*, which is published in English in Taiwan.

Imperial Tea Court

1511 Shattuck Avenue, Berkeley, CA 94709

(800) 567-5898

www.imperialtea.com

Roy Fong has been selling tea and educating tea lovers for a very long time. Those who rue the closing of his Imperial Tea Court in Chinatown, San Francisco, can be consoled by the fact that he has reappeared in Berkeley, California with a tea shop, a tea house, a website, and a blog.

Jing Teashop (online only)

www.jingteashop.com

Sebastien Leseine and his wife, Jing Lu, are located in Guang-dong, China, but ship to the United States. Because they are in China, they have the opportunity to purchase small quantities of special, seasonal Chinese teas, which they offer for sale on their website. Visiting their website frequently will reward one with a good education in Chinese tea. Lovely classical Chinese porcelain tea wares are available as well.

Seven Cups

2516 E. 6th Street, Tucson, AZ 85716

(866) 997-2877

www.sevencups.com

Zhuping and Austin Hodge have an amazing website with a wealth of information, including several tutorial videos of Zhuping discussing and steeping various teas. They sell Chinese teas exclusively, which they purchase directly from tea makers whom they know and respect. Teas are clearly marked with copious details and information. Seven Cups also offers annual tea tours to China.

Shan Shui Teas (online only)

www.shanshuiteas.com

Brian Wright specializes in Taiwan oolong and Korean green teas. Korean green teas are especially difficult to find in the United States, and Brian's selection is a refreshing welcome.

Silk Road Teas (online only)

www.silkroadteas.com

Ned and Katherine Haggerty purchased Silk Road Teas from the legendary David Lee Hoffman. Ned continues the tradition of traveling to China regularly to visit the tea fields, tour the tea factories, renew bonds with tea colleagues, and search for the very best teas. The Haggerty's selection is comprehensive and well chosen and represents China's best and vast repertoire of handmade tea.

Tea Habitat

21B Peninsula Center, Rolling Hills Estates, CA 90207

(310) 921-5282

www.teahabitat.com

Imen Shan offers a range of Chinese teas, but her specialty is Feng Huang Dan Cong teas from Guangdong Province, China. She also is a source for authentic clay Chazhou tea stoves. Imen is impressively knowledgeable about her beloved Dan Congs but beware: these teas are intoxicating.

Tea Trekker

65 King Street, Northampton, MA 01060

(413) 584-5116

www.teatrekker.com

This is where you will find us, Mary Lou and Robert J. Heiss, and our selection of pure, premium leaf tea and tea wares. While we specialize in fine Chinese tea, we are equally proud of our selections of Assam and Darjeeling teas and other specialties from far-flung regions of the tea world. We directly import many of our teas from China, India, Japan, Nepal, and Taiwan, and we proudly blend all of our blended teas in the store each week. Customers love it when they catch Bob creating a new batch of our very popular Earl Grey tea. When you are in the area, please stop in and say hello.

Teance Tea Room

1780 4th Street Berkeley, CA 94710

(510) 524-2832

www.teance.com

Anyone who has visited Teance can immediately envision the marvelous tea tasting table in the center of the room where one can enjoy flights of tea for sipping and comparison. Owner Winnie Wu was one of the first tea specialists to emphasis source and seasonal specificity in Chinese teas, and she writes eloquently and passionately about tea and her thoughts and experiences with tea on the Teance blog.

ACKNOWLEDGMENTS

Morning tea, afternoon tea, anytime tea . . . what would life for many be without tea? It keeps us company when we are drinking alone and draws friends to gather together around the kettle to share a cup.

It is reported that the Qing Emperor Qialong (r. 1736–1795) once commented on the importance of tea by saying, "The country cannot do without a ruler for one single day. But the ruler cannot do without a cup of tea for one single day."

No matter what name it has—*çaj, čaj, çay, chá, chah, chai, chiya, choy, shahtea, tee, teh, tēja, teo, thé, thee, ti, tiè, trà, tsa, tsai*—this satisfying beverage that we know as tea, steeped from a simple and unassuming leaf, can variously refresh, calm, fortify, soothe, and energize.

The tea trail winds along numerous paths, connecting countless places. We wish to acknowledge all the passionate tea drinkers and tea enthusiasts of the world who, by imbibing in their beloved cup, contribute to the health of the tea industry and ensure its continued vitality. The cultivation and manufacture of premium tea requires the best efforts of vast numbers of workers, all of whom will have "a little more rice in their rice bowl" as more people discover the pleasures of a divine cup of tea and tea-drinking veterans continue to explore new tastes and sources beyond their familiar favorites.

INDEX